THE SUN IS MY ENEMY

The
Sun
Is
My
Enemy

One Woman's Victory Over a
Mysterious and Dreaded Disease

HENRIETTA ALADJEM

PRENTICE-HALL, INC.
Englewood Cliffs, New Jersey

Library of Congress Cataloging in Publication Data

Aladjem, Henrietta,
The sun is my enemy.

Includes bibliographical references.
1.   Lupus erythematosus—Personal narratives.
I.   Title.   [DNLM: 1. Lupus erythematosus, Systemic—
Personal narratives.   WR 152 A316s   1972]
RL100.A4   616.5'4   72-6949
ISBN 0-13-875955-3

10 9 8 7 6 5 4 3

FOREWORD

Seventeen years after I came down with lupus, my eye caught the word "Help!" in an old magazine. It appeared in large letters over a small picture of a woman's face which was covered with gauze. Below the picture I read, "I suffer from an obscure human ailment—I have systemic lupus erythematosus. Can anyone, please, help me!"

I read the words several times. First I thought it was an ad or some gimmick aimed at sensational effect. But I realized immediately that I was wrong. No one could exploit a sickness as painful as lupus. I understood only too well the woman's helplessness, and felt compassion and sorrow. In the ensuing month her plea haunted me. Off and on, whenever I reflected upon my own miraculous remission from lupus, I would hear her cry for help with the surreal clarity of a dream. In an effort to locate her, I contacted both *Newsweek* and *Time* magazines—but the news item could not be identified.

It occurred to me that if I could write a detailed account of my own lupus story, perhaps that suffering woman and others might read it and benefit from my experiences. My own life had been changed in 1956, when Jordan, the nephew of friends of ours, had told me his story. He had had lupus in remission for over thirty years. Before I had met Jordan, all five doctors whom I had consulted had told me that SLE was a rare disease of obscure origin, fatal, and often of short duration.

But how does one sit down to put her miseries on paper for the public? My nature recoiled. I convinced myself that if I dedicated the story to all the women who have been smitten by systemic lupus erythematosus, perhaps I could go through with it. Women have been stigmatized by an illness with an unpronounceable name, an unknown cause, and a poor prognosis. And for too long they have been the unwitting victims of their own environment—of the sun, of drugs, of who knew what? Talking like this to myself, one day I began to write, delving into the painful memories, singling out the facts that had relevance to the case, anxious not to overdramatize the situation.

In writing this manuscript, I have compressed the events of twenty years into a story requiring only a few hours' reading.

Some of the dramatis personae bear fictitious names; others who remained closer to the flow of events appropriately appear as themselves. In recreating the dialogue, I have quoted from memory and trust I have not misrepresented their opinions or intentions.

I have presented my case history of systemic lupus erythematosus day by day, as I have experienced it.

H. A.

Wellesley

ACKNOWLEDGMENTS

I feel greatly indebted to all my doctors, and there were many; they all were counselors and healers.

I should like to express my deep gratitude to Professor George V. Smith of the Harvard Medical School for whom I have special warm feelings; next, I should like to thank Dr. Antoine Fried for his friendship and the moral support he has given me and my family during my illness. My thanks also to Dr. Louis K. Diamond for his kindness and wisdom in knowing who would best handle my case; to Dr. George W. Thorn, who, as chief of medicine, was the catalyst who mobilized brain power and resources of Harvard's Peter Bent Brigham Hospital toward the relief of my suffering; to Dr. Frank H. Gardner, warm, gentle, and understanding physician whose exuberance, intellectual curiosity, and stamina gave me hope during a seemingly unending series of crises; to Professor Liuben Popoff of Bulgaria and to Dr. and Mrs. Floyd H. Black.

The manuscript, several years in the making, needed the encouragement of persuasive and critical people such as Mr. David McCord, poet, historian, and Peter Bent Brigham Hospital trustee; Otto Zausmer, associate editor of the *Boston Globe;* Dr. Phin Cohen of the School of Public Health; Dr. Chester A. Alper of the

Blood Grouping Lab at Children's Hospital Medical Center in Boston; and Murray Chastain of the Harvard University Press.

I feel grateful to my two English teachers, Miss M. Eleanor Prentice of Wellesley College, who tutored me patiently for two and a half years, and Mrs. Eleanor R. Collier of Boston University, who continued my English education in the same spirit for another year.

With the help of my young friends, David Willard, Heather MacPherson Wiske, and Claudia Stone, I managed to fight the lost battle against dangling participles, prepositions, and unruly English spelling.

Without the love of my family, particularly the unwavering optimism and devotion of my husband, I can't imagine having survived the ordeal.

H. A.

CONTENTS

"Bless what there is for being."
                    —W. H. Auden

INTRODUCTION

This book of human drama in extremely human terms has in it the contending life to save contending lives. It was written expressly and humanely with that alone in mind. But let the unafflicted reader who has never even heard of SLE—*systemic lupus erythematosus*—be assured of losing not one decimal of all that here contributes to a personal but unpretentiously heroic story in 150 pages of distinguished, often memorable, prose. It is an absolutely authentic story, fully but never intrusively documented; yet it reads at times like running water and, in the long surprising sequence of crises, like vivid flashes out of Helen MacInnes, Dorothy Sayers, Ngaio Marsh. All in reverse, of course, for this concerns the *saving* of a life. From the very subtle beginning one is continually aware of an ineluctable will pragmatically at work against tremendous odds. The reader with no more medicine in his head than had the loose-jointed shaman of the plains will wonder more than once: can this author possibly survive to write this book?

In a word—and no introduction should be much longer than a word—*The Sun Is My Enemy* is a minor miracle which may well prove to be a major miracle. For without question it is a miracle of recorded fact: a case history in which the patient is the recorder, almost unaware of how she manages to make the reader feel the fortitude, expanding spirit, and imagination with which she fought and won a battle normally on schedule toward a lethal end. She fought it for some twenty years, in and out of hospitals, on two continents, under the best of medical and patient care, straight on and up and into a happy turn of fortune. It is a

miracle likewise in the telling, for Henrietta Aladjem was born in
Bulgaria, and did not speak English until she came to the United
States to marry in her twenty-fourth year. I was in possession of
all these facts when asked to read the early manuscript in 1970. I
opened it one night in the aftermath of a chronic case of what the
Greeks call *apatheia*. I think now of something Thoreau once
said: "Not that the story need be long, but it will take a long
while to make it short." I shall never forget my initial reading. It
was the instinctive style of this non-native writer almost as much
as the story itself that astonished me. Readers of Isak Dinesen
and Freya Stark will know what I am trying to say: Dinesen, a
Dane, because she triumphed over English; Stark, an English
stylist, because she triumphed over Arabic.

   Lupus—Latin for *wolf*: a disease by the very sound of it; lethal
by identification with the predator. *Lupus erythematosus,* fur
thermore, for there are several forms of this cutaneous ravager.
Erythematosus, from the Greek, means literally "to be red";
hence the dreaded so-called "red butterfly" rash which appears
on the face of the sufferer, spreading across the bridge of the nose
out into wings on the cheeks. The conservationist in me regrets
that the historic concept of the wolf in Russia, Canada, and the
United States, among other countries, as essentially evil, per-
mitted the use of his name for what in fact *is* evil. Man in his
organized stupidity is still relentless in killing off one of the
nobler animals once secure and useful in a balanced nature. You
have only to read Lois Crisler, Farley Mowat, and Rachel Carson
to realize that wolf, the animal, and lupus, the disease, are two
very different traffickers in death.

   Now lupus, to my uncertain knowledge, has only within the
last few years been noticed in the public press. The following
paragraph from the Manhattan Chapter, Lupus Erythematosus
Foundation, Inc., is worth reprinting for its capsule analysis from
the medical point of view:

   "When the *Collected Stories* of Flannery O'Connor won the
National Book Award for fiction this year, it was brought to light
that the late novelist was a victim of the disease which has baffled
the medical profession for more than a century. The origin of
SLE is unknown and, at the present time, there is no known
cure. It is a disease of the connective tissue, and the most

widely held belief as to the cause is that it is a disorder in the body's production of antibodies. Something has gone wrong with the immune system so that the person becomes allergic [sensitive is a better word] to some part of his own tissue."

What must have brought the matter to light was the profound introduction by Robert Fitzgerald, poet and translator, Boylston Professor of Rhetoric and Oratory at Harvard University, to Flannery O'Connor's *Everything That Rises Must Converge* (Farrar, Straus and Giroux, 1967). His detailed description of O'Connor's case of lupus is worth looking into. It should be considered, furthermore, in the light of what Henrietta Aladjem notes in one of her references at the end of this book: namely, that Flannery O'Connor's father suffered from lupus. Somehow this adds a further question mark to her own statement in the last chapter: "The possibility of a genetic background for my disease stood out in my mind."

It is clear that Henrietta Aladjem was born with the courage to face that later ordeal of twenty years. She put herself on trial in a fateful hour. From childhood on she had yearned to go to America. When she left her home and parents in Sofia—single, twenty-three, and America-bound; and how memorable, how *strong* and memorable, is the telling of that in Chapter 11— she left on 3 March 1941, the very day the Germans entered the city. She took the unusual route to America, as Kipling had some fifty years before her, but for a very different reason. Her touch-points on the map were Odessa, Kiev, Moscow, Vladivostok, Tokyo, San Francisco, New York, Boston, and Cambridge. Besides her personal belongings, she carried a bag containing fifty-two books. She will tell you that she was always a reader; but the flavor of her prose will do the same. Many years before she spoke English she had read in translation the now unread Thomas Mayne Reid (1818-1883); and her youthful first hero was a Reid red Indian. She had absorbed Masefield and Verlaine by way of entering poetry—she has the instinct of a poet, knowing as well as Auden, whom she reads today, that poetry "survives in the valley of its saying." She spoke and speaks Serbian, Bulgarian, Roumanian, and French. She learned to speak English by working for five years in the Russian Department of

Harvard's Widener Library, supplemented by library studies at Simmons College in Boston. In the main, though, she was and continues to be an autodidact. Only the self-taught ever really know, to borrow words from Wallace Stevens, "of how/Much choosing is the final choice made up."

Here is a brief passage on her departure from Sofia:

"I was cold, but I closed my eyes a little tighter, afraid that I would break the spell. I could see the train pulling out of the Sofia railroad station; that evening Mother's eyes looked like emeralds, only greener. They shone like stars bathed in tears. As I watched her, I knew I would never again see eyes so wise, so human and so tender, for they were Mother's eyes; in them I clearly saw her soul and all her love for me. . . .

"Father rushed to get me on the train. He walked with me from one compartment to another looking for a seat. I was the only girl on that train—the rest were German soldiers. Eventually, he found a place next to a window.

"When Mother saw me, her voice trembled like a leaf. 'Don't be . . .,' the whistle's piercing sound muffled the rest of her words. The train gave a jolt, another whistle and we were moving. Father found the strength to joke in those inhuman moments, hoping to bring a smile to my face. 'Don't forget,' he called out loudly, trying to keep up with the train that gathered speed. 'Act like a Boy Scout; forget that you are just a girl.'"

We live, as someone has said, in a day of safe surgery and dangerous drugs. A few years ago, after I had written a history of the first fifty years of the Peter Bent Brigham Hospital—*The Fabrick of Man*—I read a book edited by R. H. Moser (v. footnote 29) called *Diseases of Medical Progress*, frightening in its intimation of side effects unknown, which may or might appear years after the specific drug (more than any one of 250 of them) was taken. Look up your favorite antibiotic, pain-killer, or headache tablet in the glossary! You will worry more about yourself and less about what will happen to the mind of the human race in the Orwell year of 1984. When J. B. S. Haldane published in *Possible Worlds* his now famous chapter called "On Being One's Own Rabbit," he knew pretty well what he was doing; what specific personal risks he was taking. In the classic case of the present lupus survivor the list of drugs involved by trial is just as frightening as the foregoing examination of diseases of medical progress. I have noted a few, not quite so poetic as the catalogue of ships or of whales. "By now [Chapter 13] I was taking cortisone, chloroquin, potassium chloride, Serpasil, atropine, the nicotinic acid I bought in Chamonix, Pyribenzamine, and a row of vitamins—B_6, ascorbic acid, folic acid, riboflavin, and cod-liver oil concentrate." Small wonder that another lay reader of this manuscript made the following observation, perfecto size, obviously unusable in the text itself. By permission of the observer, I give it here. It is an introduction *in parvo, de profundis:*

"The author can be seen as the informed and persistent consumer of medical services of the most experimental nature, a voluntary human guinea pig through necessity. Her needs are the result of an illness of the most devious and insidious nature—an imposter of a million disguises. Her hope and optimism give her the courage to pursue treatments others would shun. But she does not choose death by passive acceptance. She chooses to live, no matter how arduous the trail."

Incurable optimism is the great analeptic. This lupus patient had it. When the chips were down, Sir Winston Churchill had it

Of *dramatis personae* in *The Sun Is My Enemy,* in the leading role the lupus victim is naturally dominant. But the doctors, particularly three or four of them, are each in his own way very powerful characters. So are those hospitals strong in the art of patient care. They and these constitute a part of undying connective tissue, as in history is Harvey Cushing through his correspondence with his young blind patient operated on five times in all; or Sir William Osler in so much of what he wrote on doctor-patient relationship in his still unequalled *Aequanimitas.*

Well, if Dr. Frank H. Gardner, Physician-in-Chief of the Presbyterian Hospital in Philadelphia, Dr. George W. Thorn, Physician-in-Chief, Peter Bent Brigham Hospital (1942-1972), and Dr. Louis K. Diamond, Professor of Pediatrics, Emeritus, Children's Hospital in Boston, become familiar to the reader, so will the old man, "ashen in the sunlight," who sat by the Chamonix entrance to the tunnel under Mont Blanc when it was nearing completion. He sat not with *les mains croisées et la bouche fermée.* He was the far-gone victim of silicosis: a Peer Gynt character in the flesh, another old man of the mountains, whose "lantern on life's long pilgrimage of fear" was going out. His tragic case was clear-cut. Henrietta Aladjem's was not. Yet it seems even to a layman that sulfadiazine and acetaxoleamide (Diamox)—on evidence however slender—may have caused or unmasked her SLE. But let this remarkable story, containing, *pari passu,* two remarkable dialogues, unfold itself.

So what *is* this book which will surely give "perspective and courage" to doctors and patients struggling with lupus? Is it indeed a novelette, a documentary, witness literature, animated diary, a quasi-medical work? To me it is simply one uninterrupted declaration of a strong, intelligent, and courageous woman in love with the gift of life. "Nature," the unbelievable Mr. Professor Dr. Popoff said to her in Lyon, "when she turns against you is a strong enemy." But the author can be aphoristic too. "I should say *we* won. I was a good patient."

David McCord

THE SUN IS MY ENEMY

Primum non nocere.[1]
−*The First Law of Medicine*

HOLLAND

"YOUR PATIENT DOESN'T have a chance. Her last LE prep was positive.[2] Her kidneys have collapsed sixty percent. What more evidence do you need?" The authoritarian voice with a sonorous Harvard accent sounded nightmarish behind the door of my hospital room at Peter Bent Brigham. The narrow metal bed I was lying in reeled in a spinning room. In this fraction of a moment, I reached within for my center of balance, and learned more about myself than I had in a lifetime. How could I have known that day that a few years later my rare and little-known disease would be arrested, and I would again be able to enjoy an active life; that fifteen years after the onset of my lupus I would be free-lancing as a reporter for the *Boston Globe* from Paris during the "Month of May" in 1968?

My first symptoms of systemic lupus erythematosus[3] appeared in the second week of June 1953. My husband, a wool merchant, had to go to Holland on business for a few weeks. We combined his business trip with the family's summer vacation. Our children were still too young to enjoy such a trip, but we decided to take them along. Martha, almost one and a half, was in diapers; Ingrid, almost five and quite mischievious; and Arthur, six and one half, at the very peak of his exploring curiosity, had to be chased all the time.

I remember vividly the five of us riding in a taxi after we had spent a sleepless night in a stuffy train compartment from Boston to New York. Shortly after we drove through the Holland Tunnel, the S. S. *Nieuw Amsterdam* appeared in full sight. The children's growing excitement infected their parents. For an instant I thought that I felt dizzy but suppressed the feeling.

"It is hot." My husband scanned my face and pointed to a thermometer on a building we were passing—it read 84 degrees. Moments later, I started shaking and shivering with chills that seized me with uncontrollable fury. As our taxi stopped, I was violently nauseated. After that I felt better. The date was June 14, 1953. I have never been able to recall how we boarded the ship or how I descended below deck to our two cabins. I do remember the steward's friendly greeting; he recognized us from our previous voyage. The sturdy Dutchman had courtly manners and a sense of humor as well. He ruffled up the hair of the two older children, then counting one, two, three, he congratulated us on the new addition to the family. After we were settled in our cabins, I felt much improved. I attributed the whole episode of my upset to the tension, the heat, and my usual discomfort when riding in an automobile for very long. Under normal circumstances the nine-day sail to Rotterdam would have been a real pleasure, but my nausea persisted, due, I felt sure, to the motion of the boat. I never thought to take my temperature.

I looked forward to visiting Holland again. We had spent the entire summer there in 1947, right after World War II. Then, the city of Rotterdam lay in ruins. The center of town was totally razed, like a metropolis without a heart. Odd remnants of walls stood here and there, preserved for future use; the debris had been cleared and the streets cleaned. Now, crossing the city, my husband and I marveled at the changes six years had brought. The city was indeed returning to life, but there was still much to be rebuilt. Arthur and Ingrid, who were sitting in the front seat with the driver, repeatedly asked him the same question, "What happened to that house?" and the answer would always be the same: "The Germans burned it!"

Ingrid was first to notice a badly bombed cathedral and asked, "What happened to that church?" And the driver replied again, "The Germans burned the church!"

"The Germans must have wanted to burn God," Ingrid said, examining the ruins with big, serious eyes.

"Given a chance, they would," the driver mumbled. As we left Rotterdam and approached Schevingen, where we were to stay at the Witte-Brug, it was my turn to speak out when I saw the newly planted woods outside the city. Six years ago, the forests were burned to the ground.

The moment I entered the hotel, vapors of fresh paint hit my nostrils, giving me an instant headache. That night everyone was restless; Martha, in particular, cried all night. Toward morning I took her temperature. I couldn't believe it read 105 degrees. Red welts covered her body. A month before leaving West Newton, the children had had chicken pox, which Martha had caught last. Quickly, I remembered that ten days before the chicken pox appeared, she had come down with purpura,* and her condition had become aggravated by infectious mononucleosis.† The pediatrician had told me that both conditions could cause serious complications with chicken pox. I had never seen a delirious child before, and I nearly lost my mind waiting for the Dutch doctor. He assured us that Martha would be all right in a couple of days. He was right—Martha did get better, but I was completely exhausted.

---

*Purpura: A disease that is characterized by the rupture of blood vessels with leakage of blood into the tissues.

†Infectious mononucleosis: A self-limited probably infectious disease that presents with fever, upper respiratory symptoms, and swelling of the lymph nodes.

June, that summer in Holland, was cold and very windy, more like late October or early November in Boston. The headache I got the day I entered the Witte-Brug never left me. Our Dutch friends said that most visitors unaccustomed to the winds of the low-lands were so affected. The headache would subside when the wind diminished.[4]

The wind never diminished. The headache increased. On a Tuesday morning, Mrs. Van Voorhees, the wife of an executive of a large spice concern, called to remind us of the invitation to their cocktail party the following afternoon. As I held the phone I panicked—I couldn't speak. I could not find breath to utter a sound. Eventually, I managed to whisper that something seemed to have happened to my voice.

"Oh, dear! What a time to get ill." Mrs. Van Voorhees sounded heartbroken. She confessed the party was to be given in our honor, and everyone was so eager to meet us. "Please be well by tomorrow," she pleaded. In the same low tone, I promised to attend the affair. In the morning I stayed in bed until I had to dress for the party. As I glanced at myself in the full-length mirror on the bathroom wall, I was glad that in a frivolous moment I had bought the Jacques Fath pink chiffon gown at a sale in Boston. The four layers of sheer petticoats in all the shades of the rainbow renewed my feminine vanity.

The Van Voorhees' large drawing room was crowded and smoky. The air, too thick to breathe, smelled strongly of coarse Dutch tobacco and heavy French perfume. The very instant I stepped into the room, I felt as if I were riding on a stuffy bus with nothing to hold on to. I looked around for a place to sit down, but all the chairs had been removed for the occasion.

An exotic-looking woman in a mink jacket was leaning against the grand piano at the other side of the room. She watched me with a sympathetic eye; her face was streaked with perspiration just like my own. I became puzzled why she should swelter in that fur.

The man who stood beside me reeked of wine and garlic. With busy eyes he followed my gaze and whispered close to my ear that Mrs. So-and-so was half Indonesian. For a split second, my short, red-faced neighbor, the floor, everything around me seemed to sway before my eyes. "She is charming," I heard him say as I regained my composure. This time I nodded and he went on to tell me that in the past, many clandestine relationships had taken place between Dutch men and Indonesian women. "These girls," he breathed again in my face, "make exquisite lovers, often excellent wives, heh . . . heh. . . . They never learned how to repress their instincts."

I looked at him absently, not sure I could get through with the party. Only stubborn determination held me on my feet. I searched in the crowd for my husband, planning my escape. A matron on my right started talking to me faster than I could follow. She was telling me that everyone at the party was dressed according to price and style to show how successfully each husband was managing his directorship. She even said that the woman by the piano had to sell an oriental rug, a family heirloom, to buy her mink jacket for this occasion. My new acquaintance, barely pausing, said that my husband and I belonged to the "in" crowd, even though we were not of Dutch origin.

Curious, I couldn't resist asking her to explain. According to her, our two husbands had reached their present position by appointment, in contrast to most of the other husbands in the room, who began their careers right after high school as stock clerks. When my husband appeared, I told him in a voice sounding quite unlike my own, that the room was stifling and perhaps we ought to go. He didn't hear my last words, but led me to introduce me to a Dutch man with whom he had played tennis many years ago—in Bulgaria, of all places.

The party had started with cocktails and endless trays of hors d'oeuvres, followed by turtle soup and morsels of pheasant and countless other Indonesian specialties—a veritable dinner. But the food tasted bitter to me. My throat felt constricted. I could not swallow a bite. As soon as the coffee was passed around, as if on cue, the guests made their excuses and started leaving. By then I could hardly walk. "How do you feel?" my husband asked me in the car.

"Giddy," I said and took off my shoes with difficulty. In the few hours I stood through the party, I had started to hate my own feet. The I. Miller rose-de-bois satin slippers, so divine when I had tried them on in Boston, pinched me beyond endurance. Now, looking down, I was amazed to find my feet swollen to double their normal size.

"From now on you'll have to learn how to say no when you don't feel well." My husband watched me from the corner of his eye.

"That would be very hard," I found the strength to tease. "Remember, I am the girl who can't say no."

"I do." He put his arm around me and repeated once more, "You'll have to learn how to say no! That's all there is to it." Later, more than once, I remembered his prophetic warning when I was tempted to overtax my energies. Back in our hotel room, while he showered, I sat at the edge of my bed, too sick even to undress. During the night I experienced a peculiar and frightening sensation in my arms, or rather no sensation in them at all—they had vanished in the darkness. Seized by fear, I reached for the electric switch; everything felt normal again. I persuaded myself that whatever was wrong with me was similar to whatever Martha had had in the previous few days, and I fell asleep again.

In the morning I awoke with a temperature of 102 degrees. My whole face was swollen; I was bothered by a sharp pain in my nose, which, the children remarked, looked red. Ingrid brought me a small mirror and I saw a bright red and slightly swollen nose. Briefly I lost my speech again. Horrified, I succeeded in calling Dr. Vandam. He appeared in the late afternoon. With a solemn expression he made a diagnosis of erysipelas.*

"Erysipelas?" my husband struggled with the word. "What does it mean, Doctor? Is it serious?"

"Well, yes and no," the phlegmatic Dr. Vandam took his time. "We used to call it St. Anthony's Fire." His thick lips stretched in a faint smile.

"It still doesn't mean a thing to me," my husband glanced at him impatiently.

"Erysipelas is triggered by an organism of the same origin as that which causes scarlet fever and other infections," the doctor explained and settled more comfortably into the old-fashioned armchair. With a sigh he unbuttoned his tightly fitted brown tweed jacket, allowing his large stomach to protrude like a ball of grease. "It's an old troublemaker well described by Hippocrates, Galen, and Celsus. . . ." He pronounced the last words with obvious satisfaction. I smiled at his last remark and complimented him on his knowledge of the ancient Greeks and Romans.

"She'll be all right," he told my husband, "but keep the children away from her for the next few days."

I read my husband's thoughts. "How could one possibly keep three little children away from their

---

*Erysipelas: A contagious, infectious disease of skin and subcutaneous tissue, marked by redness and swelling of affected areas, and often with fever, chills, and general weakness.

mother in two tiny hotel rooms with an adjoining bathroom?"

Dr. Vandam thought I might go to a hospital but almost immediately rejected the idea. "They won't take her," he said. "The hospitals still fear the infection getting close to the surgical wards. Your best bet is to take care of your wife for a few days right here in the hotel, then return to the States and have her seen by a doctor there." With that, he wrote a prescription for sulfadiazine*[5] with instructions to take it for eight days, and he left. Dr. Vandam gave me no clues whatsoever that I was about to embark on a fifteen-year battle for my very life.

I had no idea that his prescription for sulfonamide might unmask for the second time a disease which I was harboring in my system. I did not dream that all the suffering I was to endure would lead to medical research,[6] that doctors would question the sulfonamides as a potential menace for lupus-susceptible persons, and urge preventive medicine.

Lying in bed feverish, I recalled that I'd had erysipelas once before, in 1939, in Sofia, shortly after my eighteenth birthday. On a skiing trip, I had fallen and bruised my left ankle, which had become infected. I spent a month in the hospital. The drugs that Dr. Karamichailov had given me then made me deadly sick. I wondered if sulfadiazine was a derivative of that earlier medication.

My thoughts drifted. The hospital in Sofia came alive for me again with images of corridors smelling discomfortingly of disease and decay. My first morning out of quarantine I took a walk and saw in the room next to mine a young boy sprawled flat on his back in bed. The image of his face flitted through my mind. I recall him

---

*Sulfadiazine: An anti-infective drug—one of the sulfonamides.

vividly! In the semidarkness, his mop of bright red hair gleamed like a burning light around his emaciated cheeks.

Later that day, I paused by his door and chanced to meet his delirious gaze. Congestion had built up in his lungs, making respiration difficult. He acknowledged my presence with a heave of his chest. I could tell he was suffering unbearable pain. My heart was terrified; surely I was witnessing the last spark of life flickering away. A spindly resident took my arm and helped me back to bed. He explained gently that the boy had been in a car accident and all the organs in his lower abdomen were smashed. Gangrene had set in. . . . The stench was from his decaying flesh. On his way out, the young doctor mumbled, "In a few days he will be in a coma."

"But that's inhuman," I cried after him. "His eyes are telling you that he is dying, and he is begging you to help him get it over. You must do something to end his suffering."

"You mean kill him?" the resident glared.

"There must be another word for that. . . ."

"Not in my language," he shook his head stubbornly. "Nature has her ways, young lady. Who are we to interfere?"

After he left, I had buried my head in the pillow, trying to understand nature. . . . That had been so long ago. A few years later when I was so violently ill that in a moment of desperation I begged one of my doctors to put me to sleep, I could hear the voice of the Bulgarian intern in the back of my mind—"Nature has her ways."

Following Dr. Vandam's instructions, we found a Dutch girl, through the hotel office, to help keep the children away from my room. My husband attended to me, applying cold Epsom salt compresses to my face and coaxing me to drink liquids. The high fever lasted for four days. I just could not keep the fluids down.

The trip back to New York was trying. On the second day, a terrific storm developed. The waves heaved as high as seventy feet, and for forty-eight hours nobody was allowed on deck for fear that he might be washed away. I remember the whole family lying in bed, seasick. With the portholes closed, the air was stuffy and heavy. The children cried constantly, frightened by the rolling motions of the boat. As the storm increased, the ship's physician, followed by a steward, came into our cabin. The steward placed a tray of sliced bread on the dresser.

"Try to eat some bread," the doctor smiled at the children. "It will help settle your stomachs. I wish I could offer you something more," he said turning to my husband and me. He left us saying that all the passengers were sick, and most of the crew were not feeling too well, either.

The steward winked at Arthur. "Cheer up, fellow— weather predictions are good for tomorrow."

When the door closed, Arthur, impressed by the doctor's uniform, asked what the captain of the ship had wanted. I told him that he was only the doctor and had promised that we would feel better by tomorrow. "He suggested that we eat some bread," I said, and joked that today was sick day on board ship—everybody was celebrating the same holiday by feeling miserable, even the sailors.

Ingrid sighed, "Who knows, maybe by tomorrow there'll be a different celebration."

"Yah," Arthur made a sour face, "tomorrow might be fun."

Early next morning the storm subsided. The steward came to open the portholes, letting in a rush of fresh air. Sunlight flooded our cabins. My husband and the children eagerly dressed to go on deck. But my own nausea persisted. As the ship plowed on toward port in

New York harbor, I felt so ill that I thought to myself, "If someone would only throw me overboard—what a relief that would be."

BACK IN THE STATES

AND SO I RETURNED to the States to start a long siege of lupus erythematosus. Fortunately, I was unaware of how ignorant the medical world was about this devilish disease. For, in truth, I was half dead, and if I'd known that three long years would elapse before any diagnosis was reached, and another seven years of experimenting on top of that, I might have lost my spirit.

We reached our home in West Newton, Massachusetts, on the twelfth of July, five weeks after we had sailed on the S. S. *Nieuw Amsterdam.* The first few days at home I felt better; the redness of my nose subsided, and so did my temperature. But getting out of bed in the morning was a torment. I lay under the blanket waiting for someone to bring me two aspirins and a cup of hot tea to resurrect me. Then I could not dress until I soaked in a warm bath to loosen my joints. I was determined to keep going and to do my chores even though after a few hours I was forced to go back to bed and lie down prostrate.

Our next-door neighbor, Dr. Antoine Fried, was our family physician. When he had examined me several times, he suggested that I enter Newton-Wellesley

Hospital for a thorough checkup. After four days of hospital tests, I returned home feeling no better. None of the hospital reports contained any diagnostic surprises. The sedimentation rate* was slightly elevated, Dr. Fried said, and the white count was somewhat low but with a normal differential. He suspected a low-grade infection and didn't see cause for any alarm. "You might benefit from a few vitamin B_{12} injections," he said and proposed to institute them for a week or two. "In any event," he added sympathetically, "take it easy for a while and don't overexert yourself." He felt confident that the whole thing would blow over. The results of the tests had strengthened his feelings that there was nothing very wrong with me. In case my discomfort persisted, he had plans to send me to a specialist to be tested for arthritis. He ended each visit with a smile of sincere reassurance.

By nature, I have always been active, enjoying sports and outdoor living. In Bulgaria, I climbed the mountains winter and summer and loved to play a good game of tennis. But, most of all, I liked baking myself in the sun. Now, for the first time, staying in the sun disagreed with me; the direct sunlight bothered my eyes, and I did not tan anymore.

One afternoon Martha ran out of the yard, and as I tried to catch her, I found that I could not run. My legs felt heavy, as though stuffed with cement. I could barely walk. Just to test myself, the following day I tried to run across the yard, but I just couldn't. For the first time I feared that my condition might be really serious. It was the end of July.

A month later my eyes started feeling peculiar all the time. I had the same old feeling about them I'd had

---

*Sedimentation: The settling of red blood cells to the lower portion of a volume of blood which has been treated to prevent clotting.

about my arms in Holland the night they'd seemed to
have vanished in the dark. Now, my right eye felt as
though it were an empty socket. Both eyelids were
swollen with fluids. The right one was slightly dis-
colored. It turned a ghostly white, but only for a few
hours at different times of the day. I made an
appointment with a Dr. Sload, (a fictitious name), an
eye specialist in Boston. He examined my eyes with the
patience of Job but couldn't find anything wrong. He
said that I wouldn't need glasses for another ten years or
longer. As I left his office, he actually congratulated me
on my excellent eyesight. Nevertheless, my eyes continued to feel bizarre.

When summer turned into fall, my waning strength
could not cope with the house and the children, so we
hired a young Norwegian girl to live with us. Bjorg
assumed her duties with a sense of responsibility and
eagerly assisted me in every way possible. With her help
I somehow managed to keep the household running.
Ingrid and Arthur were in school now, which helped. I
could live a semblance of a normal life if I were careful
and didn't exert myself.

When the cold weather set in, my joints became
extremely sensitive. One day I noticed a new symptom.
If I leaned on my arms just below my elbows,
twenty-four hours later tiny pale pink lumps about the
size of a kernel of corn would appear around the spot of
pressure. If I used scissors, similar nodules appeared
around my finger joints where the scissors had pressed.
If I walked for any length of time, the bottoms of my
feet turned red and hurt terribly. I tried to explain this
new development to Dr. Fried, but each time I made an
appointment, by the time I kept it, the lumps had
disappeared. It was very embarrassing; I couldn't understand it at all. After I made three such appointments, on
my last one, Dr. Fried joked that he was scaring the

lumps away. "I do have such effect on certain disorders," he chuckled. That day I left his office feeling more than foolish. Was I losing my mind? I wondered.

FLORIDA

SINCE CHRISTMAS VACATION was approaching and I was still feeling miserable, my husband suggested that I try a warm climate for a couple of weeks. "Take the children and Bjorg to Florida," he said. "There is nothing like a ray of sunshine when one's joints ache." I agreed, and he promised to join us for as much of the time as he could.

We started on this trip on a clear Friday morning in mid-December. When we left the house, at seven o'clock in the morning, Commonwealth Avenue was covered by a few inches of fresh snow—the sun glared icy-blue.

"The sun looks frozen," said Ingrid.

"It shines like a crystal ball," said Arthur.

"It's covered by ice cubes," added Ingrid, who had climbed onto my lap. "It must be shivering like Mommy." She snuggled closer.

By the time we reached South Station, more icy shivers ran through my body—the cold clung to me with incredible sharpness—my blood felt frozen. On the train, the change from snowsuits and boots to light summer clothes delighted the children. Bjorg bubbled in anticipation of seeing semitropical country.

The next day, I got off the train in Miami tired and listless. I could scarcely lift my legs off the ground to enter a taxi. In the bright semitropical sunlight, I developed a prompt pupillary reaction* that forced me

---

*Pupillary reaction: Constriction of the pupil in response to light which may be painful in inflammatory disorders of the eye.

16

to shade my eyes with my hand until I could buy a pair
of dark glasses. Bjorg seemed bewildered by the artificial
garlands of Christmas decorations on Collins Avenue.
From every store songs like "White Christmas" and
"Jingle Bells" blared out to us. The sweltering Santa
Clauses ringing bells in front of gas stations cut sad
figures amidst the palm trees. This was Bjorg's first
Christmas away from home and she began crying. When
she had controlled her emotions, I could hear her telling
the children that in her village in Norway, Christmas was
a spiritual experience—nothing so tangible and vulgar as
it seemed to be here. I fully agreed with Bjorg with whom
I felt an affinity at the moment. I, too, was homesick.

As it turned out, in Florida, instead of feeling better
as I had hoped, I felt worse. My acute discomfort and
intuition began to alert me to the dangers of ultraviolet
light. However, the sun still tempted me on days when I
felt better and once I went to the hotel solarium for a
few hours. During that night I developed a mild
temperature and slept poorly. The following morning
my body was completely covered with a bright red rash
and my face had broken out in blue blotches. Toward
evening two angry red sores appeared on my forehead.
Each one was half an inch in diameter, and they were
sensitive to the touch. The waitress in the dining room
commented that I had "sun poisoning"—a term I had
never heard before, but by now I was willing to accept
any diagnosis. After ten days in Florida, instead of the
two weeks we had originally planned, I put Bjorg,
Martha, and Ingrid on the train and I took Arthur on
the plane with me—a first flight for both of us.

One hour after we were in the air, I had to remove
my shoes; my feet had swollen to a grotesque size. When
Arthur remarked a couple of hours later that Boston
with all its lights looked like a Christmas tree, I sighed
with relief to be home.

WEST NEWTON

AT LOGAN AIRPORT, the moment I stepped off the plane, a cold, icy wind enveloped me in a new blanket of pain. My head whirled and my stiff joints grew stiffer. I struggled to reach the terminal with Arthur tugging at my skirt. My husband exclaimed with alarm at the eruptions on my face. "I couldn't tolerate the sun," I said, trying to sound casual.

"That's strange," he observed my face more closely. "All your life you've loved the sun so much." In the car, he urged me to call the doctor at once.

First thing in the morning, I went to see Dr. Fried. He, too, was troubled by my worsened condition. My swollen legs and ankles seemed to puzzle him more than the eruptions on my face. He prescribed acetazolamide.*[7] The drug reduced the swelling but did not eliminate it completely. The headache, nausea, and dizziness persisted; I felt almost as sick as I had on the boat coming back from Europe. When Dr. Fried suggested that we increase the dose of acetazolamide, I felt reluctant to follow his advice. I told him I had a weird feeling that drugs were worsening my affliction.

In the days that followed, I developed a twitching of my limbs and an impossible itch all over my body. The itch was driving me out of my mind. My two little girls were taking turns in scratching my back.

---

*Acetazolamide: A sulfonamide diuretic (causes increased urine formation or excretion). Trade name Diamox.

Next, an angry rash appeared on my arms. Dr. Fried decided to send me to a skin specialist in Boston. The Boston man prescribed a powder and a thick paste to be applied daily to the rash. After each application, the eruptions worsened. The ultraviolet light*[8] that he used on it increased the rash, the itch, and the pain throughout my body. I sounded like a madwoman when I tried to explain to Dr. Fried that whatever I was taking by mouth or applying to my skin was killing me.

Dr. Fried and I discussed the matter further. He declared that, once and for all, we had to determine the exact nature of my problem. "You have so many complaints suggestive of rheumatoid arthritis, I think it's time you saw a specialist." He recommended Dr. Zenith[9] of Massachusetts General Hospital in Boston. "I'll make the arrangements right now." He picked up the telephone and made the appointment for four o'clock that same afternoon.

I parked the car in front of Dr. Zenith's office on Commonwealth Avenue near the Boston Public Garden, which was about seven miles from my home. The temperature hovered around zero. My limbs ached in the worst way imaginable—my knees wobbled. Wondering if I could make it to the front door, I rested against the outside wall of the building. I managed the front door. Then I had to face the elevator. Opening that door was impossible—I had no strength left to lift my arm. I wrestled with my tears until a man appeared and rescued me, and we rode up together.

Dr. Zenith, a slender man in his midforties, noticed immediately my weakened state and rushed to offer me a seat. He said that I shouldn't be out on such a cold day. I admitted that I couldn't struggle against the

---

*Ultraviolet: That portion of the spectrum of sunlight which tans the skin.

assault of the weather. On cold days like this I felt like a
car with a frozen motor. "But even when it is warm, I
don't feel any different," I said.

"I can understand that," he offered in a sympathetic
tone. After he completed the historical phase of the
interview, Dr. Zenith asked me to lie down on a wooden
table with a comfortable two-inch mattress, and began
the physical examination. He spent over half an hour
examining my muscles, my swollen joints, and checking
my reflexes. My reflexes were satisfactory, my lungs
were clear, the liver and spleen felt of a normal size.
When I was seated again in front of his desk, he
casually inquired if I had any problems other than my
physical ones. I must have looked rather surprised, for
he hastened to ask, "Are you depressed?"

"By the disease, you mean?"

"Well, what we usually mean by 'problem' is"—he
hesitated—"do you get along with your husband?"

I shrugged slightly, failing to see the connection.

"Do you have any money problems?" he persisted.

"Money problems?"

"Can you pay your bills?" He observed me for a
moment, then dropped the subject.

When my examination was over, Dr. Zenith suggested
that I take two aspirins* every three hours. "It's
important to take them regularly," he advised. "Take
the aspirins with a glass of milk," he added, and
promised that the salicylate would alleviate my pains.
After two days of taking sixteen aspirin tablets per day,

---

*Aspirin: In 1763, it was discovered that an extract of the willow bark
was effective in relieving the pains of rheumatism. Willow extract owes its
therapeutic efficacy to a substance that is called salicylic acid—from the
Latin name for willow, *salix*. A chemically modified form, acetylsalicylic
acid, is marketed under the name of aspirin. For reasons still unknown,
aspirin proves helpful for relieving pain.

my stomach turned sour. The milk, instead of helping, gave me cramps and diarrhea.

At my next visit, Dr. Zenith made a tentative diagnosis of rheumatoid arthritis. He said that my sedimentation rate was elevated, which suggested possible inflammation in my system. I also had a rather low white blood count and there was no albumin* in my urine.

He leaned over his desk and noted down some more studies that he wished me to have made. When he had finished writing, he handed me the slip of paper. "Here are some of your appointments I have arranged. The results of these studies should help us make a more definite diagnosis. Your first appointment is tomorrow at Massachusetts General Hospital in the Arthritic Therapeutic Department," he said and stressed that the hydrotherapy there was superb. The application of water, such as whirlpool baths, and the exercise should help indeed. He remembered to ask me how I had managed with the aspirins. I told him that the aspirins made me sick and so did the milk.

"The milk, too?" He seemed surprised. "Milk intolerance is uncommon in this country." He shrugged and suggested that I try Gelusil tablets instead of the milk. "It's an antacid control," he explained.

I asked him what the elevated sedimentation rate meant. Dr. Fried had mentioned that, too.

"An elevated sedimentation rate is usually associated with inflammation or some underlying complication or infection," he said. "But, in your case, I don't anticipate anything serious. Your hematocrit, hemoglobin, serology, and all your other blood values so far are normal." Dr. Fried had reported that my myasthenia

---

*Albumin: "White protein"; an important protein of human blood serum which may be found in the urine in diseases of the kidney.

gravis* test, thyroid tests,† and chest X rays were also normal.

In the car I looked at the slip of paper Dr. Zenith had given me in his office. I read:

> Wednesday + Friday—Mrs. J., Physical Therapy
> Hematology routine‡ LE?

The letters "LE" did not stand out on the slip of paper. In fact, they appeared quite innocent. But through the ensuing seventeen years, they were to lose their innocence and become instead a dreaded gate holding life or death to me.

---

*Myasthenia gravis: A disease in which nerve impulses are not properly transmitted to the muscle cells. As a result, muscles all over the body become weak.

†Thyroid tests: Basal metabolism, radioactive iodine uptake—tests to determine whether the thyroid gland is over or underactive.

‡Hematology routine: Routine tests to count the cells of the blood. The LE cell is a white cell that has eaten the nucleus of another white cell; the latter appears as a blue-staining spot inside the first cell.

a chronic civil war within the
body. . . .[10]

—DR. MICHAEL CRICHTON
Five Patients

When the vital forces of the body
are in mutual disagreement one says
that the disease is difficult to
cure.[11]

— *The Yellow Emperor's Classic*
of Internal Medicine

MASSACHUSETTS GENERAL HOSPITAL

MASSACHUSETTS GENERAL HOSPITAL is located in downtown Boston near the Charles Street Jail and the West End Bridge. Approaching the bridge from the Cambridge side, I tried to remember if this were the one referred to by some Bostonians as the Longfellow Bridge after the lovely poem "The Bridge." As I drove across the Charles River, I dredged up the lines, "I stood on the bridge at midnight,/As the clock was striking the hour. . . ," and promptly missed my left turn at the busy rotary.

Inching my way with the traffic, I landed not at the hospital but in Scollay Square, right in the heart of Haymarket. Never had Boston seemed so colorful to me, so Bulgarian. I found a strong likeness to market day in Sofia. That's how a section of town used to look on Fridays when the farmers brought their produce for sale. Here, too, the sidewalks were lined with old-fashioned grocery stores and the cars could hardly move

between the pushcarts heaped with fruits and vegetables. The market men made lots of noise in broken
English instead of Bulgarian. When I stuck my head out
the car window, I detected at least three foreign
accents—Greek, Armenian, and Italian. The air smelled
of trotters marinated in bay leaves and vinegar, and I
whiffed some stale blood. Lately I'd become terribly
sensitive to odors. The slightest smell could make me
nauseated. A feeling of disgust swept over me as out of
the rear of his truck, a man pulled a large carcass
half-wrapped in brown paper. The sight brought to mind
how, as a growing girl, I had hated to go with Mother to
the market, for that always included stopping by the
butcher's shop. It made me sick to look at the butcher's
white apron splattered with blood . . . and more blood
dripping from his meat counter into a chipped enamel
bucket on the floor.

Only last week, Dr. Fried had asked me if I ate a
balanced meal. I did now, but for years in Bulgaria I had
refused to eat meat. It was a fad, Mother said, and
Father teased me that I was doing it to show my
support for Mahatma Gandhi, my hero. But now that I
looked back on it, I was more inclined to blame
Abe Rott, the butcher, and the glazed eyes of the
lambs that stared at me from every corner of his
shop.

I reached the parking lot of the hospital by 9:20
A.M., ten minutes before my appointment. The walk to
the main entrance was endless and the distance from
there to the Arthritis Department ridiculous . . . a
healthy person would collapse. In the waiting room a
ten-year-old boy watched me with curious black eyes
from his wheelchair. His father, a sturdy-looking man
dressed in Esso coveralls, offered me a piece of gum
after he had given one to the boy and put two in his
own mouth. I took it.

The black woman sitting on my right appeared well

until I saw her fingers curled like eagles' claws. I imagined they were twisted by pain, mercilessly. The thought made my flesh creep. The black man beside her glared into space with heavy red eyes as though he were attending a funeral. In the few minutes I sat there I began to feel like one of them already, and I was getting depressed. When a red-headed nurse came to the door and called my name in an Irish brogue, I was ready to flee from the place in horror. I followed her hesitantly through a ward swarming with cheerless, arthritic patients. As I walked along behind the nurse, breathing in the patients' pain and helplessness, I felt defeated.

"Suppose I become a cripple, too? Suppose my fingers curl in like the black woman's? Suppose, suppose . . . What's the use, forget it," I snapped at myself. Through one more door the exercising gym was crowded with more crippled and dejected people—a nightmare. "Dante must have had a similar sight in mind when he described his walk through the lower realms of the next world," I told myself. "How else could he have imagined such misshapen bodies, such tormented expressions, such eyes so full of doom?"

"You look as if you expect to see the d-i-v-i-l," the nurse said as we entered a room divided into cubicles by curtains.

"You mean Lucifer?" I mumbled, trying to keep up with her fast pace. She pointed to a bed table for me to lie down. Shortly after I stretched out on the uncomfortable table, a tall heavy-set intern came to question me about my symptoms. While he spoke to me, he checked my reflexes. After a few minutes, he moved on to the next cubicle where a black man was groaning. The nurse took over. She showed me for half an hour how to exercise every muscle and joint in my body while lying flat on my back. On my way home, I felt more depressed than ever.

During one of my visits to the Hematology Laboratory, I overheard two technicians talking. They were unaware of my presence in the next room.

"Golly, I feel sorry for that woman with the foreign accent—the one we did the LE prep on," one said. "It was positive."

"Positive?" the other asked in a strange way. Then I heard her again: "I don't know what an LE cell is."

The first answered, "It stands for lupus erythematosus. The doctor said it's a horrible disease—it's incurable."

"I've never heard of it."

"You are not the only one. The doctor said he'd seen only a few cases in the past few years, and they were all in the terminal stages."

Although the voices at the time remained implanted in my mind, I did not then associate myself with the "woman with the foreign accent." At my next appointment in his office, Dr. Zenith received me in a friendly way, but I felt a slight uneasiness in his voice when he began to tell me about the results of my blood tests.

"Something in your blood is puzzling us," he said. "We found a few cells which are suggestive of SLE. The test raises some questions of systemic involvement."

"SLE?" I repeated the letters, not hearing the rest of Dr. Zenith's words.

"That's short for systemic lupus erythematosus[3]," he said, then looked at me for a moment. "The cells we found are only suggestive, not diagnostic, of lupus. We shall repeat the test."

I was stunned. The conversation I had overheard at Massachusetts General flashed through my mind. "What does lupus erythematosus mean?" I asked, feeling as if I had started to die already.

Dr. Zenith spread his palms. "Frankly, we don't know much about the disease—not yet, anyhow. We think it has a tendency to alter blood vessels and connective tissue; it could affect the kidneys. . . ." He shrugged a little. "I wish I could be more specific. For the moment, the affliction is not recognized with much accuracy. I guess with lupus, the first diagnostic act is to suspect the disease."

"Is there any treatment for the disease?" I asked, terribly worried.

"Not really," he said. "If the condition becomes acute, we manage to control it with cortisone."*

"So, it's incurable," I mumbled to myself. Then I suddenly asked him if I could be given cortisone.

"No, no, not at the moment," he hastened to answer. "Truly, we spent hours the other day examining your blood again, but we couldn't find another abnormal cell."

He had an ascetic angular face with clear penetrating eyes. It was hard not to believe him. He reminded me to continue with the aspirins, do the exercises they taught me at Massachusetts General, keep the no-salt-added diet and try to rest as much as possible. Later he helped me get on the elevator, and before he closed the door, he said, "Sometimes all of a sudden the patient begins to feel better for no special reason at all. I've seen it happen with other patients."

Several months went by. My sickness seemed to go on forever. Pessimism was not part of my makeup, but as matters grew worse, I began to lose hope and started to feel insecure. "How does one keep from despairing?" I kept asking myself. Was I ready to accept defeat? Was I going to give in to melancholy?

Dr. Fried came periodically to our house to give me

---

*Cortisone: A potent hormone of the adrenal glands; the pure compound was first discovered in adrenal secretion by Dr. Edward C. Kendall of the Mayo Clinic and by Dr. Reichstein of Basel, Switzerland, simultaneously in 1936. It is now synthesized as a pure chemical.

the vitamin B_{12} injections. I suspected that the good man kept coming to keep up my morale and prevent me from developing a neurosis. Everyone in the family grew fond of him and he returned our feelings. The children anticipated his visits as much as I did. He used to bring them a few sugar candies in small envelopes, pretending to be their doctor. And my husband's face always brightened after he returned from walking Dr. Fried to his home next door. He, too, needed some moral support.

During this time, my system began to retain fluids and I felt dizzy. The radiators in our house were the old-fashioned kind—painted a bright silver—and if I looked at them for very long, their shape appeared distorted. The same would occur with the geometric design of silver and gold in the wallpaper. The bizarre floating sensation and difficulty in focusing seemed like an hallucination. I could not bring myself to mention the radiators or wallpaper to anyone. In a voice full of anguish I told my husband, though, about another maddening experience. "I know that I am not crazy," I said emphatically, "but you may wonder after I tell you. If I reach for a book or a plate, I sometimes feel that they move further away and I am not sure that I can make the contact. I know that I am not crazy," I repeated, "but I feel like I'm going out of my mind."

"Stop saying that you are not crazy," my husband assumed a joking tone. "That's what crazy people do. They are usually the last ones to admit it." Then he became serious. "There must be a reason for your peculiar symptoms. Explain all this to Dr. Fried. But," he teased some more, "don't insist that you are not crazy."

I burst into tears. "I don't want to see a doctor again. They don't seem to know what's wrong with me. Every time I am given a medication, I feel worse instead of better.[12] Anyway, what do I have to lose?" Just as my husband was about to speak, I rushed on, "And furthermore, with all the odd symptoms I am experiencing, I don't want to discuss my illness with anyone. Whenever you or I try to explain what's ailing me, we become so involved and so foolish sounding—it makes me feel uncomfortable. More than that, it makes me feel crazy." The last words came out as a screech.

"We won't talk about your sickness any more if that bothers you." My husband took my hand. "But please stop worrying about it," he remonstrated. "You don't owe an explanation to anybody. So there." He looked as distraught as I was.

However, after a few more days of misery, my husband became increasingly worried and insisted I go and see a blood specialist, and I reconsidered my decision.

> *To discover the agent of disease and*
> *death depends on a patient piecing*
> *together of many seemingly distinct*
> *and unrelated facts developed*
> *through a vast amount of research*
> *in widely separated fields.* [13]
>
> > −RACHEL CARSON
> > *Silent Spring*

CHILDREN'S HOSPITAL MEDICAL CENTER

OUR PEDIATRICIAN WAS a renowned blood specialist and a professor of pediatrics at Harvard Medical School. Through the years, we had built a steady friendship and I valued his judgment. After much deliberation, I phoned Dr. Louis K. Diamond.[14] I asked him if he would consider doing some blood testing on me to determine possibly whether or not I had lupus erythematosus. I told him of Dr. Zenith's findings in my blood. Between suitable pauses, he asked me a few questions to give himself time to reflect, then said yes, he would see me the following morning.

Dr. Diamond was also the associate Physician-in-Chief of the Children's Medical Center in Boston and his office was located on the fourth floor of the main building of the hospital. At ten o'clock the next morning Dr. Diamond welcomed me, eager to hear more about my condition. His face reflected a sad gentleness that I assumed he had acquired through his many years of working with suffering children. With his courteous manner and impeccable dress, he gave the impression of an old-fashioned European gentleman.

"I am glad you called me," he said, holding a chair for me. "You look well," he added amiably. "I see no lupus."

"I am afraid I've panicked," I murmured.

He looked down at my face and smiled. "I never would have suspected you of panic."

"It's an impossible situation," I said. "I am getting tired of seeing so many doctors. Besides Dr. Fried, I have seen a skin specialist, an eye specialist, a thyroid specialist, a myasthenia-gravis specialist, and a rheumatoid-arthritis specialist—I am reaching the point where I don't want to see another doctor."

He didn't reply to that but went behind his desk and sat down himself. He pulled out a pad of paper from his desk and for a moment remained quiet as if wondering how to begin. His office overlooked a terrace full of pigeons. Two well-fed birds came close to the window and stared at Dr. Diamond in an expectant way.

Dr. Diamond jotted something down, and then opened his diagnostic questioning by asking how I felt.

"I feel tired, dreadfully tired. At times I can barely lift my arms."

He nodded with a sympathetic look. "I'll be more than happy to do a complete blood analysis on you. But I must warn you that, since you are a grown woman, I can conduct only a limited examination. Anyhow, we'll talk about this later," he said and then asked. "Besides being tired, do you have any other symptoms?"

"God, yes. I feel dizzy most of the time." Dr. Diamond wrote this down. Suddenly I was anxious to tell a doctor everything that was wrong with me. When he looked up again, I said, "In the past year I have been more susceptible to infections than I can ever remember."

"What do you mean by 'infections'?"

"I have a constant sore throat—a very peculiar one. It hurts and it doesn't! It's hard to describe."

Dr. Diamond looked up from his notebook.

"And I have recurring bouts of nausea. This plagues me more than anything else. I can't stand it!"

"Any skin problems?" He focused his eyes on my face.

I described the redness that had appeared on the exposed parts of my body. "The V-neck in particular has turned an angry red, suggesting sunburn." Instinctively I unbuttoned my dress a little to show him the redness. This seemed to puzzle him. We were quiet for a moment.

Then Dr. Diamond asked, "Did you have proper nourishment as a child?"

"What do you mean?"

"Did you have enough to eat?"

"Yes, as far as I can remember I was a well-fed child. Bulgaria used to be famous for growing fine fruit and vegetables," I added, a little puzzled by his question.

He looked up briefly from his pad of paper, then turned to a fresh page and looked at it as if he were reading something important. "All right," he said, "let's have a short history of your family. Are your parents living?"

I nodded. "They are quite young and healthy," I assured him. "My father is fifty-nine years old and Mother is fifty-six.[15] They married very young," I added when he raised his eyes.

"Any brothers or sisters?"

"Just one brother, a year and a half younger than I."

"In good health?"

"As far as I know. He has always been healthy."

"Any grandparents still living? If not, what did they die of?"

"On my father's side, my grandfather died at age

forty-five of a heart attack. His wife lived to be sixty-eight. She died of asthma. I loved that grandmother dearly," I went on in a burst more intimate than I should have. "I was only ten at the time of her death, but I can still recall my distress. Mother used to say that I took after Maia spiritually and physically. Maybe I also inherited some of her allergies, although I have never had asthma."

Dr. Diamond smiled discreetly, then bent down to write as I continued.

"On my mother's side, my grandfather died of a heart attack, too, and my grandmother lived to be very old—she had her last baby at the age of forty-nine." Dr. Diamond chuckled and asked if I were conscious of any special diseases among other members of my family. All I could remember was that my mother and father had each lost two brothers with TB. "Mother always overprotected us as children against colds, for fear that we might catch the disease."

"You must be getting tired." He put his pen down on his desk and asked if I would like a glass of tomato juice before we continued. I nodded and he went out and brought back two large glasses of cold tomato juice. "Just a few more minutes of questioning," Dr. Diamond said when he put his glass down. He wanted me to recall some of my childhood diseases.

I remembered mumps and chicken pox and when I was eight, double pneumonia and hepatitis* which kept me from school for half a year. I told him I used to have bronchitis and a chronic running nose that I was constantly reminded to wipe. I also remembered that at age nineteen I had a deep abscess under my right arm which had to be opened under general anesthesia, and I told him of the skiing accident after which I had

---

*Hepatitis: Inflammation of the liver.

developed erysipelas. "I felt dizzy all the time," I said and stressed once more the miracle drugs I was treated with. "The ankle has bothered me ever since," I paused for breath. "Several weeks after the skiing episode a sore the size of a quarter appeared on the right calf of my other leg. That oozed pus for months and months. I still have the mark."

"That's interesting." Dr. Diamond became more animated. "Do you have any idea what those miracle drugs were?"

I didn't. In Bulgaria, doctors did not discuss such matters with their patients. I mentioned the erysipelas I'd had in Holland at the onset of my present disease and the sulfonamide the Dutch doctor had given me. "Somehow every time I am given these drugs, instead of feeling better, it seems to me I feel worse." I listened to myself repeat the same words that I had spoken when Dr. Fried had administered the acetazolamide.

Dr. Diamond did not interrupt me at all. Only when I finished, he said, "Tell me more about the sore on your leg."

"A question of TB of the bone was raised," I recalled, "but meanwhile the sore healed, and nothing further was done about it."

"I'll look at your scar later when I examine you." Dr. Diamond leaned back in his chair. "Then what happened?"

"I came to this country and was married, and it seems like I have been seeing doctors continuously ever since. I am beginning to feel uncomfortable talking endlessly about myself. It must sound to you like a dull autobiography."

"With an uncommon condition like yours, the doctor assumes the role of a detective, and any detail, however trivial or remote, may hold the key to the solution of the mystery. Let me tell you"—he smiled—"before we come up with a correct diagnosis you'll probably have to repeat your story more than once." He meant every word—as I found out countless times later.

"You arrived in this country, you were married," he read aloud from his notes. "Did you have normal deliveries with your children?"

"More or less. I was married five years before Arthur was born. I needed a small operation to conceive." I paused to remember what followed immediately after. "After the delivery, a kidney infection developed."

"Did that clear up right away?" Dr. Diamond asked.

"I had a fever for a while, then I was given . . ." I suddenly stopped.

Dr. Diamond looked up from his pad of paper.

"I was given something to combat the infection and I developed a horrid-looking rash. I had lumps all over my scalp."

Dr. Diamond wrote with hurried strokes, then said, "Go on."

"A year and a half later Ingrid came along. This time the bleeding continued for some months, so I had to return to the hospital for a D and C."* I heaved a long sigh and went on talking in monotone. "Two years later, I had a miscarriage. But in four months I was pregnant again with my last child. This pregnancy began with bleeding, which eventually stopped. The delivery was extremely difficult. Labor had to be induced and I was given several blood transfusions. Martha turned out to be a healthy eight-pound girl with a wonderful disposition."

"I know," he grinned. "She is a charmer. But how did you feel when you returned home from the hospital?"

"Not too well," I shrugged. "Walking was very

---

*D and C: Abbreviation for dilation of the cervix and curettement of the uterus.

difficult, at times impossible. Phlebitis* developed in both legs. The skin became ulcerated[16] and a year later, the veins had to be stripped." I cringed at the memory. "The incisions did not heal properly and staphylococcal infection set in and lasted for over six months. That brings me just about to the beginning of my present difficulty," I said, then reluctantly repeated to him the current symptoms that I already had gone over with Dr. Fried and Dr. Zenith.

A petite nurse walked in with a tray full of tiny tubes. She drew an ounce or so of blood from my arm and pricked my finger for some smears. As she did so, Dr. Diamond phoned Dr. Zenith's office and asked if he could see the positive LE prep I had mentioned. Dr. Diamond could not hide his annoyance when he was told that one of his technicians at Massachusetts General Hospital had lost the preparation. A few minutes later, a trim, vivacious young woman entered and introduced herself.

"I am Dr. Heally,[17] Dr. Diamond's assistant." She extended me a friendly hand. "I am here to help with your examination."

Dr. Diamond indicated that Dr. Heally would take over. I followed her to a small room next door. She helped me undress, then pointed to an examining table, and told me to lie flat on my back. She moved a chair close to the table and started the customary tedious examination. I had to answer more questions—as she went over every inch of my body. When she finished, she covered me with a crisp white sheet so that I could be seen only from the chin up, and called in Dr. Diamond.

He came into the room and felt the lymph nodes on my neck, then lowered the sheet just enough to put his

---

*Phlebitis: Inflammation of a vein.

hand first under one arm, then under the other, to check for more nodules. It took some skill to manipulate the sheet so that my spleen, liver, and abdomen could be felt without exposing an unnecessary inch of flesh. At the end of the examination, he confessed that he hadn't examined a grown woman since his medical school days, which made Dr. Heally laugh and me turn crimson.

Dr. Heally reported to Dr. Diamond that I appeared to be in good shape. Except for a bunion on my left foot and the redness of the V of my neck, she hadn't come across anything impressive. We made my next appointment for Saturday morning, two days later, when Dr. Heally was to measure the sugar level in my blood. Dr. Diamond said by then all my other blood values should be back. I left his office with a glimmer of hope.

On Saturday, Dr. Heally was already waiting for me in Dr. Diamond's examination room. "How do you feel?" she greeted me with a friendly smile.

"Tired, just plain tired."

She confessed that she, too, was worn out, having studied all night for her medical board exams. "There are literally thousands of facts to remember! It's murder!" she exclaimed. I agreed that some exams were sadistic in nature and should be modernized, along with other things in the educational system.

"God should hear you in a hurry, before I collapse from the tension."

Dr. Diamond peeked in and asked how his grown-up patient was, then hurried off before I had a chance to answer. An hour later I was in his office once again. This time we sat down to talk at the other end of his large room. Seeming more comfortable, that corner had a green leather sofa and two matching easy chairs. Dr. Diamond informed me right away that my blood picture was good. "I did all the tests myself," he said, "and everything looks fine." He sounded genuinely pleased. "The cell we found is not the typical LE cell; there is a slight morphological dissimilarity. We come across such cells more frequently than the true LE cell." I could feel my breathing quicken. "In my opinion, you don't have systemic lupus," he said and nodded to confirm his words. "You might have a related condition to lupus, but even that will have to be determined by more specific tests."

"Dr. Diamond," I suddenly asked, "what does an LE cell look like?"

He asked me to move closer to the round coffee table and drew a small circle on the cover of an old *Life* magazine. He carefully filled in some shadows inside the circle. "That's roughly how an LE cell looks under the microscope," he said. "Some of the white cells, have large abnormal bluish lumps inside them. We call these cells LE cells."

"You are a fine teacher," I remarked.

"I like teaching," he replied, "and I like to explain to my patients all I can." He adjusted his glasses with extra care and said, "Recently we've found positive LE cells in patients who are hypersensitive* to penicillin, tetracycline,† and the anticonvulsants.‡ In some instances, penicillin can produce lesions of polyarteritis nodosa,§ a disease resembling lupus," he explained. "And at Robert Breck Brigham Hospital, over twenty percent of the rheumatoid arthritic∥ patients have LE cells. They were admitted as arthritic cases, but probably have something that is at least related to lupus."

---

*Hypersensitivity: A form of allergy generally mediated by antibodies, a special group of blood proteins.
†Penicillin and tetracycline: Antibiotics.
‡Anticonvulsants: Drugs used to reduce frequency of convulsions.
§Polyarteritis nodosa: Inflammation of the large arteries.
∥Rheumatoid arthritis: A chronic disease of the joints.

This was the first time that I had heard of Robert Breck Brigham Hospital. It is the arthritic hospital in Roxbury, and not to be confused with Peter Bent Brigham, which was next door to Children's Medical Center. "The presence of an occasional LE cell is not reliable evidence of SLE," Dr. Diamond continued. "In several diseases that overlap with lupus, we can now find LE cells. Several other conditions can mimic systemic lupus, and some criteria are merely suggestive of the disease and should not be applied dogmatically." I was absorbing every word. Suddenly there was hope. "I believe that things will turn out all right," he said and settled more comfortably in his large leather chair.

"I must find a name for this sickness of mine," I said.

"If you must," he smiled, "we could still call it a relative, something of a cousin to lupus. . . ." His voice became firmer when he added, "However, your condition is not something that you can manage by yourself. That would be foolish!" He sounded for a moment as if he were talking to a child. "You need a skillful man who will become interested in your case and be willing to spend lots of time on it." He observed me for a moment, waiting for my reaction, then went on, "I have a doctor in mind, but for the next year he is engaged in special research in Puerto Rico. But we cannot wait a year. For now, we should get in touch with Dr. George W. Thorn[18] at Peter Bent Brigham Hospital. I hope that he will consider taking your case." When I didn't openly react, he continued, "Dr. Thorn doesn't see many patients; he, too, is engaged in research. His field is endocrinology."*

I had no idea what endocrinology was, but I agreed to see Dr. Thorn because of my implicit trust in Dr. Diamond's judgment.

---

*Endocrinology: The study of the glands of internal secretion.

Pleased, Dr. Diamond wrote down the names of some vitamin pills for me to take: folic acid, B_6, ascorbic acid, and a few others, all to be taken in large doses for a few weeks. I was to continue to see Dr. Fried and get the vitamin B_{12} injections. Since I had complained about taking aspirins, he told me to try Bufferin for my aches. "If that doesn't work, Alka-Seltzer might," he chuckled. "Both are actually aspirin buffered with excess sodium bicarbonate."

As I left the Children's Medical Center, I walked a little straighter. The fright that had hounded me since I had overheard the two technicians at Massachusetts General lessened. The solid enemy of lupus became fragmented in my mind into several diseases of various strengths. Today each one of them was worth fighting. It seemed easier to think that I could overcome a condition related to lupus than the disease itself.

Dr. Diamond's promise of eventual recovery stimulated a feeling of expectancy. I was beginning to feel as if forces of life were generating new energy in my system. I repeated to myself that one should assert life even at the edge of despair. Crossing the street to the parking lot, I recalled once more the resident doctor in Bulgaria and the dying boy. Strange! I could not think of the name of the hospital any longer, but I remembered clearly what the doctor had said. "Nature has its ways, young lady." His words assumed a special meaning for me now. And the eyes of the dying boy? I could still see them. They were burning with life. The brief look that he and I had exchanged so long ago remained a bond of compassion between us. "One should assert life even at the edge of death." I heard an echo from deep within me, and I breathed in and I breathed out a little lighter.

OUR HOUSE ON PRINCE STREET

DRIVING BACK TO Newton from Dr. Diamond's office, I crawled along at 30 mph, still dwelling on what I'd been told. Dr. Diamond had given me new hope, but I still had to find a way to arrange my life in such a way that I could spare all my strength for the family. Instinct told me that I'd have to change my modus vivendi, perhaps sell the big house we were living in. Even with Bjorg to help, the demands of the house overwhelmed me. My increasing weakness seemed to make the simple walk from one enormous room to the next almost impossible. What a dreadful thought—to have to sell our home! The idea horrified me. My husband would be most unhappy. To him the place had become a symbol, the planting of his roots in America, an anchor for his family. Besides, what Bulgarian ever thought of selling his property? A house stayed in the family for generations, complete with mothers-in-law, grandparents, and ancestral ghosts.

I thought, as I drove, of how our house must have looked seventy-five years ago when it was built by a prominent Boston Brahmin family with taste and money to lavish on details; it must have been charming then. But when we bought the old English Tudor, it was worn and badly needed repair. We enlarged and brightened the kitchen by knocking out a wall and adding a window. Two of the three bathrooms needed new tubs and showers. The ceilings on both floors were sagging in places and ready to cave in. The furnace had to be replaced, as did every shingle on the roof.

To carpet, curtain, and furnish our house to look American, yet instill a European air, took time and imagination. . . . We started by choosing Kirman rugs like those back home and hung a few paintings done by friends. We mounted the blue and white tiles that I had brought from Holland around the dining-room fireplace. For the mantlepiece, I chose the two large old jugs from my Delftware with silver mounts, gifts of Mr. Van de Vettering, one of the directors of my husband's company. I added a claret bottle and two old sack[19] jugs. The arrangement looked most attractive. So did the blue plates with their patterns of pastoral scenes now gracing the dining-room walls; the very colors of blue and white bred simplicity and gave pleasure to the eye. Most of the pieces I had dug out of shops in small old Dutch towns, and they imparted a bit of my personality to the house.

After having lived for ten years in Cambridge on Massachusetts Avenue, I now appreciated the trees, the shrubs, and the large piece of sky I had rediscovered. From my new kitchen window above the stove I could see the south wall of the garage covered by climbing flesh-colored roses, each flower the size of a peach. Beyond, at the edge of the lawn, the wooden fence was covered by a mantle of scarlet rosebuds. The heavy garlands of tiny beauties hung loosely to the ground. The rhododendron bushes by the front walk were huge. From the living room the blossoms appeared like clouds of pinks and mauves and deep purples.

The house that had been at first too formal, too somber, too large, and too dilapidated suddenly became too beautiful for words . . . but was still too big and taxed my strength. A horn blared and I jumped in my seat.

"Watch your driving, dummy!" a woman shouted

from a car. She angrily waved a white-gloved hand at me and shrieked, "Who the hell gave you a license?" The gray sedan flew by me. I realized I was driving at a snail's pace, wobbling in the middle of the road.

A week after I saw Dr. Diamond, Dr. Thorn's secretary called me to arrange for an appointment. His office was at Peter Bent Brigham Hospital in Boston, a relatively small but very important hospital connected with Harvard Medical School.

Patients' participation based on sound medical information can be of much help to the doctor.
   —DR. GEORGE W. THORN

A bed, a patient, a doctor, a nurse, and a cook do not constitute what the French call a Hôtel Dieu in the way that Mark Hopkins, the student, and a bench might conceivably constitute a college. [20]
   —DAVID McCORD
   The Fabrick of Man

PETER BENT BRIGHAM HOSPITAL, BOSTON, MASSACHUSETTS, 1956

WHEN, THREE DAYS later on a Friday, I went to see Dr. Thorn, I came face to face with Jack, the policeman in charge of the hospital premises. I reached Peter Bent Brigham twenty minutes before my appointment with plenty of time to park, or so it seemed. I circled around the hospital more than ten minutes, but no space. Suddenly I noticed a vacant spot in front of the Harvard Medical Library with a large sign, "No Parking at Any Time."

"The bear is afraid, but I am not," I said, remembering an old Bulgarian saying, and started to park. Halfway in, I heard somebody growl loudly, "Hey, lady, can't you read?" An old and very annoyed policeman came to my car window. "Hey," he said again, "what do you think you're doin'?"

44

Despite his loud voice, the man looked more like Santa Claus than a ferocious guardian of the law. "I'm not hiding anything," I said. "I am parking."

"What do you mean you're parkin'?" his voice rose another octave. "Are you out of your mind?"

I told him that I had no choice. I had an appointment with Dr. Thorn in exactly five minutes and I intended to keep it, even if I had to break the law. "Anyway," I gave him a smile, "I have never broken the law before in all the sixteen years I have been driving."

"Oh, yes, you have," he fumed. "It's just that no one ever caught you. You can't leave the car here. We'll tow it away."

"But I will," I insisted. Choking with rage, he threatened to summon me to court for deliberately breaking the law and flaunting the fact, too. Something about Jack's expression made me tease him. I don't know where my strength came from to be funny that day. Casually, I remarked that he could take me to court, but that would not concern me; it would be strictly an issue between him and the Dutch government. "What do you mean?" He looked astonished.

Keeping a straight face, I said, "My husband works for a Dutch concern and I am driving the company's car." But then I quickly apologized for teasing him and asked him if he would please help me find a place to park.

I shall never forget the way he glared at me. He looked as if he were facing a demon, and I heard him mutter under his breath, "When I left Ireland thirty-five years ago, me ol' mother warned me—'Jack,' she blasted, 'if you go o'er the oceans an' leave me here behind, Jasus, someday you'll see the live Divil in person!' This is the day, lady. By gorry, I feel sure of it!" he said. But just the same, he helped me park the car across the way. He also had to help me climb the few back steps of the hospital. I was in more pain than ever—my whole skeleton was in agony.

Dr. Thorn, a man in his early fifties with bright red hair and a freckled face, looked more like a young intern than what he was—a world-renowned Harvard professor and the physician-in-chief of a famous hospital. When I entered his office, I couldn't walk unattended. He helped me to a chair and said that Dr. Diamond had written him a long letter about my affliction. "We'll see what we can do to help you," he said, settling behind his large desk. As he proceeded with the usual medical questions, his face radiated unusual intelligence. His mind was quick with a flair for sharp insights—he had an infinite passion for details.

In less than an hour, Dr. Thorn managed to make me feel as if I were an associate working with him rather than the object of his investigation. He demanded all my cooperation to facilitate his task. His eyes twinkled as he promised in return to explain to me all the tests that would be taken. "That's the only way you'll become a member of the team," he said, then added, "patient participation based on sound medical information can be of much help to the doctor. . . ." His magnetic personality and confident air made me think of him as a man who would stand up against the pitiless strength of nature and fire back.

Dr. Thorn had written down all the information he needed; he became quiet, as if he had run out of words. Then, in a slightly changed tone, he said, "Can you enter the hospital sometime early next week? Today is already Friday," he quickly reminded me. He studied my face, as if to reassure himself that I understood the importance of his request. When I was slow to answer, he stressed that it was vital for him to determine the functions of my kidneys. "Have you ever had a bone marrow test?" he asked. I shook my head. He said not to worry about it; it would be no more unpleasant than drawing blood from a deep vein.

I agreed to enter the hospital, but said I preferred to return home each night to be with my children. I felt it was important to maintain a normal home atmosphere for the family—they shouldn't have to worry about my being ill.

Dr. Thorn hesitated briefly. "This is not the hospital's policy, but perhaps we'll let you go home once or twice. But let's see."

I accepted his tentative promise, admiring his skillful parrying of my question.

Satisfied, he wrote something in his notebook, then looked up again. "Let me warn you about Peter Bent Brigham. It's a research and teaching hospital, and besides the regular doctors, you will have to cope with flocks of inquisitive young medical students and interns—that's how these young doctors learn."

This marked the beginning of a long association lasting over fifteen years with Peter Bent Brigham Hospital.

Just as Dr. Thorn predicted, my stay at the hospital was a unique experience. Parades of doctors, nurses, dieticians, and medical students flocked through my room from early morning until late at night. There was constant activity. I had nothing private left about me. My life history was recorded repeatedly. Blood was drawn until no more veins could be raised. Bone marrow was taken from my hip as well as from my chest. An elimination diet was instituted to determine any possible food allergies. The search for clues continued. Every morning, Dr. Thorn and his assistants stopped in to see me. I listened carefully to their brief discussions which took place by the foot of my bed.

On one of these visits, a young doctor from Utah did all the talking. His expression was unusually keen. In a

soft but confident voice, he said that in his opinion, the
sulfonamides could precipitate systemic lupus in cases
previously diagnosed as discoid lupus, a condition that
affects only the skin. He added that there was some
evidence to implicate sulfonamides in triggering other
diseases which could be called cousins of lupus.[21] The
reference to "cousins" recalled Dr. Diamond's words,
which was reassuring to me.

When most of my tests were back, Dr. Thorn related
the results to the group by my bedside. "All the tests
seem fine," he said in a light tone, "but the patient
continues to feel miserable." He glanced briefly in my
direction. "That's not very helpful, Mrs. A., is it?"
Then, almost immediately, he turned to his young
assistants. "The patient has not had any fever. She has
no skin lesions, no renal involvement; the urinalysis
came back this morning perfectly normal, too." He
cleared his throat and continued. "The EKG,* chest
film, GI series† and IVP‡ were all normal." Gazing out
of the window, he continued his soliloquy. "Blood pressure—one forty-five over eighty, no anemia, and the LE
cell preparation has been negative three times, and the
leukopenia§ persists." He seemed to dwell on this and
underscored his interest by adding. "The bone-marrow
biopsy gave no further clue to the nature of the
white-cell problem." He glanced at his notes once more.
"The white count is three thousand with a normal
differential, and the sedimentation rate is still slightly
elevated." He shook his head a little and said, somewhat
unconvincingly, "Despite all the fuss about the white
cells,[22] our findings are not impressive—nothing to get

---

*EKG: Electrocardiogram.
  †GI series: Gastrointestinal series; an X-ray examination of the esopha-
gus, stomach, and small intestine.
  ‡IVP: Intravenous pyelogram, an X-ray examination of the kidneys.
  § Leukopenia: Low white-cell count.

excited about." Then he instinctively shifted gears as if to avoid my dwelling on the obvious white-cell trouble and stated with an air of finality, "I am really pleased to find her kidneys functioning so well."

A young intern with sleepy eyes and curly black hair commented that suspicion for lupus should be attached to any girl who had sunburn like the one I had had in Florida which failed to clear in the usual time. Another intern, who spoke with a strong southern accent, couldn't see how anyone could ever pin down SLE in a case such as mine where the LE prep had been negative so many times. Further, to him the disease was even more mysterious since he had never seen a case. Dr. Thorn admitted that it was a rare condition, but pointed out that among rheumatoid arthritis cases there was a significant percentage of hidden lupus. These words also brought to mind what Dr. Diamond had told me.

The next day, Dr. Thorn called in an infectious-disease specialist on consultation. His Harvard accent was so pronounced, I mistook him for an Englishman. He also spoke fluent French. He seemed fascinated with philology and infectious diseases. He explained that at one time or another, infections had been implicated as a cause for lupus, erythema nodosum,* and other mysterious afflictions.[23] "Even though this view is no longer considered tenable," he said, "we have recently treated several patients with autogenous vaccines† with favorable results." He applied several patch tests on both of my arms, and before he left, he assured me in French that all would end well. Twenty-four hours later the TB skin test was positive, as was the one covered by the

---

*Erythema nodosum: Painful red bumps on the skin. A skin manifestation of several diseases, including lupus.

†Autogenous vaccines: Vaccines which are made from the patient's own bacteria, as opposed to vaccines which are made from standard bacterial cultures.

streptococcus patch. The latter became very sensitive and angry-looking. The possibility of hypersensitivity to streptococci,* while suggestive, had not been proved. Although I remained puzzled by these results, my hope increased.

The infectious-disease specialist prepared a vaccine which he planned to give twice a week indefinitely. Dr. Thorn prescribed small daily doses of penicillin to be taken along with 5 mg. of prednisone.† When he discharged me from the hospital, we agreed that I should see him once a week until my condition cleared up. Hopefully, that would be soon.

Throughout the year in which I was seeing Dr. Thorn and getting the strep vaccine, the disease seemed relatively quiet. Yet the throat irritation was still intermittently bothersome. I accepted the burden of a mild chronic affliction, something Dr. Fried had stressed at the onset of my disease, and I stopped worrying about the prognosis.

After Dr. Thorn had given me the autogenous vaccine for six months, I was gradually weaned away from it and all other medications except for the vitamins. At least for the time being, there seemed to be no cause for concern.

---

*Streptococcus: The round organism (coccus), a very dangerous bacterium that may cause sore throats and skin infections such as nephritis, inflammation of the kidneys, and rheumatic fever, inflammation of the heart and joints.
†Prednisone: The chemical name for a steroid hormone.

... and like Sir William Osler he valued the importance of knowing his patient well, so he could adequately help him.

THE NEW DOCTOR

AT THE END of the year, Dr. Frank H. Gardner,[24] the hematologist* whom Dr. Diamond originally recommended, returned from Puerto Rico. He accepted my case. Thenceforth, I was to see him once every month. A tall, pleasant-looking man, Dr. Gardner possessed the same interest in detail as Dr. Thorn, and like Sir William Osler,[25] he valued the importance of getting to know his patient well so he could better help him.

Dr. Gardner had a way of drawing me out—he gave just enough of himself to create a warm two-way relationship.

The hematology lab at Peter Bent Brigham was at the rear of the hospital. From the front entrance I used to pass through a senseless labyrinth of stuffy corridors with innumerable heavy doors which I was too weak to open. One day I counted seven such doors while I walked closely behind a heavyset nurse to whom I was grateful for patiently holding each door.

When I went the back way, I could count on Jack, the policeman, to find me a parking space and help me with the heavy door to the freight elevator.

The hematology lab consisted of several small and dingy rooms where people constantly bumped into one another. The long narrow corridor, with two wooden

---

*Hematologist: A specialist in the study of blood.

51

benches where I had to wait, was always hot and stuffy. At times, especially in summer, the place smelled of urine and other unidentified but equally unpleasant odors which emanated from the routine labs.

The room where Dr. Gardner drew blood from my arm was called "the lab." Tubes, funnels, scales, measuring cups, pots, and the like cluttered the place, giving it the appearance of an old-fashioned Bulgarian kitchen. The centrifuge in a corner of the room I fancied for months to be a washing machine. In that crowded but friendly atmosphere, Dr. Gardner did his research while training many young hematologists.

His office, across the hall, was sparsely furnished with a large desk, a leather chair with a high back to support his large frame, another chair for the patient, and an old-fashioned brown wooden examining table. The window behind the desk faced a sooty wall covered with faded ivy leaves. The depressing architecture was more than offset by the warmth and excitement of the Gardner group, all of whom helped me in one way or another to bear my ordeal. Sipping an occasional cup of coffee with Dr. Mitsu Laforet, the only woman doctor on the research team, had the effect of psychotherapy on my emotional stress. Her friendliness instilled confidence in my faltering spirit.... She and I have remained friends. Good friends.

Dr. Gardner stubbornly searched for the LE cell and watched for changes in my blood. At the time the white count fluctuated between 2500 and 4000. The sedimentation rate stayed about the same, mildly elevated. Dr. Gardner reported periodically to Dr. Thorn and Dr. Diamond about my progress. The diagnosis, for my ears, was "leukopenia*."

---

*Leukopenia: Reduction in the number of leukocytes in the blood, the count being 5000 or less.

Each day I felt better, though I was still too weak to enjoy physical activities the way I had before I became ill. I learned how to budget my strength, and my hope of getting well grew all the time. Reading and writing provided a continuing intellectual interest, as did music. My love for these pursuits had originated in my early teens. Exploring symphonies and old church music kept me in a hypnotic trance then and still does. Occasionally I delight in searching for the vibrations that stimulate the muse. Whenever I get in such a mood, I remember Mother telling me that whoever doesn't write poetry at eighteen must be a fool, and anyone who does after thirty is a still bigger one.

The wool business did well. My husband imported wool from Australia, New Zealand, South Africa, and South America, and sold it all over the world. His business interests expanded to keep pace with the medical and household expenses. My husband's attitude of "things will be better by tomorrow" sustained my incurable optimism. After a while I found myself wondering if any other kind of life existed.

Since Bjorg had returned to Norway to become a bride, we had a new household helper from Ireland. I was convinced that keeping a girl in the house was vital, not only for my own good but for the good of the entire family. The help preserved the image of a running household—meals on time, clean laundry, and a tidy home. I could save what little strength I had to do things with the children. My family never saw me as a cripple which, in fact, I was at the time.

Mary, our new girl, added a little extra to the spirit of our home. She had astigmatism in both eyes, large flat feet, and must have weighed close to two hundred pounds. Her heart proved to be worth her size. I always remember her seated at the big oval kitchen table, feasting with a crowd of never fewer than five children,

and with several contented animals lying near her feet.
The week Mary came to us, we had adopted Mev, a
handsome six-month-old golden retriever. We already
had Wuzzy, a vicious orange cat, two huge white rabbits
with stupid pink eyes, and two parakeets that never
made a sound. Mary's feet were never too tired to
attend to the needs of a child or to dance an Irish jig
with Ingrid and Martha. While nothing ethereal appeared
in her dancing, she glowed with enthusiasm and moved
with the precision of a clock. The house shook at its
foundation. Miraculously, none of my Dutch plates fell
off the wall, though at times they trembled in anticipation.

Having animals in the house pleased the children no
end. The only creature showing signs of strain that year
was Mev. An American dog by birth and early training,
it took him some time to realize that by adoption into
our family, he was expected to become a Bulgarian dog.
In Bulgaria, dogs were outdoor adventurers. They had to
earn their keep by guarding their master's house or
tending the sheep. But Mev couldn't care less what dogs
did in Bulgaria. He resented being restricted to the
kitchen and struggled for equal rights in the house. The
children sympathized with him, and eventually the
"beast" became the ruler of our household for the next
fourteen years—*Vox populi, vox Dei!*

It is termed lupus, for that it is, say
some, of a ravenous Nature, and
like that fierce Creature, not sat-
isfy'd but with Flesh.[26]

–D. A. TURNER

CANADA

NOVEMBER FOUND MY husband in Holland on business. Before he left, we had agreed to go skiing in Canada for a week of Christmas vacation. The children shared his enthusiasm for the sport. School closed, my husband returned, we packed, then children, Christmas presents, and all boarded the Friday midnight train for Quebec. The next noon we left the train under low pale gray skies and in freezing air. The family accused me of having exaggerated my description of the delights of Quebec.

Perhaps I had let myself be carried away by memories of that springtime visit when I entered via a St. Lawrence River steamer, I admitted. Martha was heartbroken. Her older brother and sister had told her that Canada was on the way to the North Pole where Santa Claus had his toy workshop. The child expected to have at least a glimpse of Prancer or Dancer, if not of Santa. Instead, the streets of the old town seemed desolate. Her blue eyes searched through the car window for gaudy Christmas decoration and Santa Clauses selling gasoline. . . . The taxi driver's radio was tuned to a soft melody. Ingrid, who was then the poet in the family, started reciting "'Twas the night before Christmas, and all through the house, not a creature was stirring, not even a mouse."

Our lodge proved to be twenty miles out of Quebec City. The tedious ride over country roads packed with ice and snow took at least an hour—it grew colder and colder. As we drove through the mountains, icy winds seeped through the cracks of the ramshackle taxi. I felt chilled to the bones. Some extra woolens next to my skin would have been a godsend. When we reached the lodge, the Laurentian Mountains were spread wide open only a few hundred feet away. The vista was breathtaking and so was the cold air. We rushed into the lodge to a pleasant surprise. Two friendly, crackling fires greeted us in both our rooms. The air smelled of birch and mountain evergreens. I stretched out on the bed with all the children bouncing around me and fell asleep until suppertime.

By the next day, to everyone's delight, the sun came out of hiding and shone for the rest of the week. On the ski slopes the wealth of snow surpassed all our expectations. For a change, the masses of sugarlike powder were not a mere nuisance to be shoveled away.

While the family skied, I roamed through the nearby hills admiring the huge pine trees. Their lush green colors contrasted sharply with the whiteness of the snow and the powder blue sky. The pine needles loaded with crystals of ice shimmered in the sun's rays— millions of iridescent baby rainbows. The day before our vacation ended, I took a long walk downhill toward Quebec. I walked for a long time as though I had forgotten I would have to return. It was a lovely day. As much as possible, I tried to avoid direct sunlight by walking hunched over under the heavy branches. I still suffered from a morbid sensitivity to light. When the sun went down, the temperature dropped below zero. The return trek seemed endless. My ears and nose were stinging, and my feet felt like sticks of ice. I could hardly lift them—only the fear of being frozen kept me moving. I reached the lodge totally exhaused.

"Mommy looks blue," Ingrid cried out.

"She's purple," Martha chimed in.

Rubbing my frozen ears, I told them that coming up the hill, the wind had turned into a dragon with fiery claws who bit into my cheeks and chased me all the way back.

"The nasty creature burned your skin like fire," Martha put her warm little hand to my cheek.

"She's teasing," Ingrid said. "There are no such things as dragons."

"Who saw a dragon?" Arthur barged in, waving a Ping-Pong paddle.

"Mommy did!" Martha's tears glittered in her eyes.

"You are silly!" Arthur scoffed and told us to hurry to the dining room before it closed. The next morning, I awoke before daylight with a splitting headache and a raging fever. My shoulders, neck, arms—every inch of me—ached. Later, when my husband brought me a cup of steaming coffee, my hands shivered so badly I couldn't even grasp the cup. Thinking that I had a severe cold, we remained at the lodge two extra days. After that, I felt well enough to start homeward.

When I returned home, I was at a loss to explain some of my symptoms. The lymph nodes enlarged on both sides of my neck, and I succumbed to nausea once more. I also developed a rash on my face which covered my nose and both cheeks in an oddly shaped pattern. My palms and fingertips were speckled with dark blue spots. The nail folds were fiery red as if hemorrhaging.

The moment I entered Dr. Gardner's private office at the front of the hospital, his eyes focused immediately on my face. I sensed his bewilderment. "What in heaven

have you done to yourself? You have a rash on your
face—a red butterfly."*

I tried to smile. "A red butterfly? Why the poetic
name for the nasty rash?"

"We call it that because it occurs symmetrically on
the cheeks and extends over the bridge of the nose. It
does look like a butterfly! Have you been in the sun
again?" He kept his eyes on my face.

"No!"

"There is a tendency for lupus to get worse after one
has been exposed to sunlight or even artificial ultraviolet
rays. You should shield your face and body from
ultraviolet light." He spoke as if I had an established
diagnosis of lupus. The word suddenly took on a special
meaning. I recalled reading that the word "lupus" meant
"wolf" in Latin. Later I learned that the disease had
been named because the ulcerations on the skin
resembled wolf bites—a common occurrence in olden
times. I reached for my pocketbook mirror to see if my
rash resembled such bites but did not take it out. Yet I
knew that I could not avoid all mirrors. I thought of the
one in the car which I so often used to look at myself as
well as the cars in back of me.

"Tell me what happened," he asked, recognizing my
anguish.

I described our trip to the Laurentians. "The sun was
strong on the ski slopes," I said, "but I made an effort
not to expose myself. I walked in the shade."

"You got the reflection of the sun off the snow," he
said. "Such rays increase the degree of the skin's
exposure. At high altitudes, the penetration of sunlight
is more intense than it appears. People with blue eyes
and light skin like yours should not fool with the sun,

---

*Butterfly rash: A form of double-wing-shaped skin rash around the
nose and cheeks indicative of lupus.

lupus or no lupus. . . ." He advised me that even on an overcast day, I should always wear protective creams or a hat. . . .

"What now?" I asked mechanically.

"We must be realistic," he shrugged a little. "Things will get worse before they get better." As he drew the usual sample of blood from my arm, he said, "Don't look in the mirror for a while."

"You must have read my mind," I murmured.

He told me that he had faith in my ability to keep up my morale. I hoped he was right, for at times I felt sure that my well of spiritual resources was running dry. Before I left, he scribbled two prescriptions: one for prednisone—a 5 mg. tablet every six hours—and another for 0.5 percent hydrocortisone ointment—10 mg. in a tube. I was to rub the hydrocortisone vigorously into the skin to make it more effective. With that instruction, I left his office.

"It will get worse before it will get better," I kept hearing his words as I emerged through the old-fashioned doors and the stately portico of Peter Bent Brigham. At the end of the front walk, no more than a couple of hundred feet, I felt drained of all energy. Sweat broke out on my face and I was overcome with dizziness. I had to sit on the curb before I could hail a taxi. A short distance away a group of children were arguing in shrieking voices. Looking at them, I wondered fearfully, if worse came to worst, what might happen to my own children.

A week later when I entered Dr. Gardner's office, he said, "You have a moon face. Your cheeks are swollen from the prednisone."

"A sun face would have been more appropriate with the butterfly rash," I said and sat down on the chair in front of his desk.

"But are you feeling better?" he asked, observing my

face. The red spots were still there, and so were the blue blotches on my palms. The glands on my neck were as swollen as ever. The one on the right stuck out like a cherry. He pulled out my file from the cabinet next to his desk and wrote down his observations.

"I am pleased with your tests," he raised his head briefly, then thumbed through some lab slips and read the tabulations aloud. "Your hematocrit is forty-three, hemoglobin thirteen-point-four, white count four-three four-oh, polys* twenty-nine, lymphs† twenty-one, BUN‡ eleven, uric acid four-point-eight, sedimentation rate twenty-two." He closed the folder with meticulous care and said, "You still haven't told me—*how* do you *feel?*"

"I feel fine," I paused. "No, as a matter of fact, I feel terrible." My lips trembled as I told him that I dreaded making an appointment for fear that I wouldn't be able to keep it. "My symptoms change from hour to hour," I said. "No matter how well I feel in the morning, I am liable to collapse in the afternoon. But, worst of all, I have a morbid feeling that I'll never regain my confidence. . . ." When I finished, I quickly added, "I am thinking seriously of selling our house, Dr. Gardner, and moving into a smaller place."

"What does your husband think about that?" His eyes never left my face.

"We haven't discussed it yet," I said. "He will need time to get used to the idea."

"I wouldn't be in a great hurry," Dr. Gardner warned. "Sometimes a patient with symptoms like yours suddenly feels better for unexplained reasons." His tone of

---

*Polys (polymorphonuclear leukocytes): White blood cells.
†Lymphs (lymphocytes): White blood cells.
‡BUN: Blood urea nitrogen. When the kidneys fail, the BUN rises, as does the uric acid.

voice sounded the same as Dr. Zenith's did at the beginning of my illness.

But the thought of selling the house had taken root in my mind. In the next few months, as my illness grew progressively worse, I decided that I could not go on living without contingency planning. Even if my health improved, our present place would mean constant dependence on outside help. In truth, my chief concern centered in my family and my desire that, were my condition eventually to take me away from them all, they should be able to manage by themselves. But these thoughts I kept to myself.

I was crying when I finally confessed one day to my husband that the hardships of a large house had become impossible. Try as I would, I had to admit that my ebbing strength no longer proved equal to the demands.

We deliberated back and forth for several months. Finally, my husband agreed that perhaps it would be better to sell the house. After a brief search, in the fall of 1957, we bought a smaller house in Wellesley, Massachusetts. Our new home was located high up on a hill surrounded by aged shady trees, lots of lady slippers, squirrels, and singing birds. I envisioned how the place would look when I could dig with my own hands and plant in the soil. . . . Here I could have a garden of my own that I could start from scratch. What fun! In my new house I knew that I could handle all my ups and downs a little more easily; here, I thought, one could never be lonely with floor-to-ceiling windows overlooking the woods and the open sky. In my new bedroom I could lie in bed and watch the moonlight creep across my garden.

Our new home was within walking distance of Tenacre Country Day School, where two of our children were second-year pupils. "No more daily driving back and forth to school for me!" I cheered when Ingrid and

Martha left in the morning to walk to school with Mev trailing after them. In the long run, my instincts for self-preservation proved right—every measure that eliminated fatigue and stress provided extra ammunition for my battle ahead.

We were scarcely settled in Wellesley when I had to reenter Peter Bent Brigham Hospital for a reevaluation of my condition. The rash on my face that had originated in Canada faded with time but did not disappear as Dr. Gardner had expected. My neck glands remained stubbornly swollen. The day I entered the hospital I had a mild fever and the ever-present nausea which made me miserable.

When Dr. Thorn heard I was in the hospital, he came to my room. He regretted the turn of events. He reflected that he had thought all my problems were solved or nearly so. . . . Dr. Diamond came every day, and Dr. Fried every third or fourth day. Dr. Gardner called in several other doctors for consultation. During this stay more medical students than before walked in to see me. Each one was curious to glimpse my butterfly rash; lupus was still such a clinical rarity. These inquisitive young men tried to palpate my spleen, liver, and kidneys with vigorous strength, as if the secret of my affliction could be found buried in the folds of my flesh. One young charmer built like a football player appeared hesitantly at my door. He watched me from the corner of his eye, as if not sure that he were in the right place. In a high-pitched voice he inquired if I were the patient he was looking for. I asked if he were expecting to find a living cadaver.

"Gosh," said the young man as he advanced close to my bed. "How would I know? You are my first lupus patient." He admitted that he was surprised to find me looking the picture of health.

His mentioning "lupus" brought a lump to my throat.

The doctors had managed to make the disease sound nebulous enough to dull its sharp edges, but still I shuddered whenever I heard it called by name.

The intern settled himself in a narrow wooden chair and jotted down: name, age, race, sex, orientation, cooperativity. He flashed a disarming smile in my direction and asked if I would help him write a paper on my case.

My gaze moved, from his gray narrow eyes that appeared ready to dissect me, to his big powerful hands. "I will oblige and tell you all you want to know," I agreed, "if you will promise not to touch me. I ache all over, and I have been feeling cold all day long. The slightest change in temperature makes me shiver."

"My grandmother is like that, too," he said with another grin. "She has arthritis and can predict the changes in the weather by the twinges in her little toe."

He consented not to examine me and we talked for nearly three hours.

The young lupus enthusiast came back two more times. I even translated two articles on leukopenia from Russian for him while I was in the hospital. Months later Dr. Gardner, who was also teaching fourth-year medicine at Harvard, commented on the student's excellent paper.

On the evening before my discharge from the hospital, I heard Dr. Gardner's voice down the hall. He was talking with one of Brigham's doctors who repeated several times, "Your patient is really quite sick. Her kidneys are severely damaged. With that degree of damage, if it is due to lupus as you suspect, it means that she doesn't have a chance."

It was obvious that they were talking about me, but for some reason had not muted their voices. After the first moment of shock, I was glad I had a chance to react to their grim words alone instead of playacting in their presence. I did not have to pretend that I was brave or frightened. I asked myself what to do... what was there to do? What would keep me going? I still had the doctors on my side, who were going to help me all they could. I still had the children to take care of. Every day I survived helped them grow a little more. Then I suddenly realized that the life I'd lived had been a full one—as my breathing eased I found some unexpected inner strength.

Dr. Gardner walked in and informed me that the latest tests showed some kidney damage. "The ability of the kidneys to clear certain substances[27] from your blood is impaired," he said. "We will have to repeat the tests, of course."

His dwelling on the word kidneys, despite the fact that it was not news to me, still had a frightful effect. My hurriedly assembled courage which the hallway conversation had inspired, suddenly disappeared. I became lightheaded. The room spun around and my mouth became terribly dry. I asked him if the kidney involvement meant that I definitely had lupus now.

He reminded me that I only had a suspected diagnosis, and in his opinion, the new findings did not alter the picture. "But," he added, "if you do have lupus, the prognosis is not hopeless—not hopeless at all. The kidney damage may possibly reverse itself. There is some hope." The last words, he pronounced in an almost cheerful tone that doctors so often adopt, knowing well that something is terribly wrong with the patient.

I tried to fasten to his last words, but I had read very thoroughly the book called *Lupus Erythematosus,*[28] edited by Dr. E. L. Dubois, a professor of medicine at the University of Southern California—it was hardly possible to survive with lupus once it got to the kidneys.

Dr. Gardner drew blood from my arm and slipped a

rubber band around the test tubes, then dropped them into his pocket. He pulled up a chair and sat down like a friend. "Stop worrying," he said. "I believe that cortisone will take care of the problem."

"Cortisone is not curative," I said.

"It's not curative," he agreed, "but the hormone* can change some of the effects of the disease before irreversible damage occurs."

From his words, I assumed that the hormones could prolong life and asked him for how long a patient with lupus lived.

"In all honesty, I can't answer your question," he said. He explained that doctors seldom followed an LE patient from the onset of the disease through to the terminal stages. The cases that came to medical attention were usually the grave, terminal ones; their life span varied from five to ten years. "Patients with lupus seldom stay for very long with the same doctor, which makes it difficult to follow the disease," he said. "People feel discouraged when the doctor is unable to provide a prompt cure and the doctor gets discouraged, too, when he cannot establish a quick diagnosis and effect a cure." He stressed that, until recently, mild lupus cases were rarely diagnosed, much less followed intensively.

When I asked him what was the major threat to life in lupus, he answered, "The kidney involvement could be a continuing threat to life."

I was to learn later that kidney difficulties are usually the least responsive to steroid hormones of all the clinical manifestations of the disease. In my case, the only way to correct my kidney condition was to eliminate the insulting agent, which still remained a

---

*Hormone: From the Greek "to excite"; hormones are chemical messengers which excite a response in other tissue.

mystery. I later learned that the kidney may be a target in the drug hypersensitivity reactions, which may unmask or perhaps "cause" lupus.[29] Even such friends as sulfonamides, penicillin, and tetracycline have been implicated as troublemakers.

The room was hot. By now, Dr. Gardner's crimson face matched the flamboyant red vest that he frequently sported under his otherwise conservative tweed jacket. He rose from his chair and told me that my blood samples would be packed in dry ice and flown to the Rockefeller Institute of Medical Research in New York City. "They have developed a more sensitive way of checking the serum protein," he said. "Let's wait until we hear from them." I could never lose my sense of the miraculous. His not being quite sure of a diagnosis injected a new hope. I held on to that hope like a child.

I told Dr. Gardner that Bulgarians have practiced diagnosis at a distance for a long time. The sick farmers had to send urine specimens to the city for analysis. As my apprehension diminished, I even managed to tell him a Bulgarian joke about a village priest who had to send a specimen to Sofia via his pretty maid. On the way, the girl slipped and broke the bottle. Frightened, she refilled a new bottle. The returned diagnosis was "Pregnant."

Dr. Gardner laughed. "I've heard about those Bulgarian farmers. They all eat yogurt."

"Yes, they do," I said, "but I have no idea why yogurt should be considered responsible for their unusual longevity."

"Yogurt is rich in lactic-acid bacteria," Dr. Gardner said.

I shrugged.

"It sometimes changes the bacterial population and has a settling effect on the stomach and intestines.[30] You should try yogurt."

"Yogurt is fermented milk. You know how I feel about milk."

"I know. You don't like it."

I shook my head. "It doesn't like me."

"Someday I'll have to test that possibility."

Dr. Gardner's sending my blood to the Rockefeller Institute marked the beginning of a long period of having my blood sent many more times to New York City, Los Angeles, California, and down east to Waterville, Maine. Dr. Gardner never missed an opportunity to listen to another opinion from an authoritative colleague, and he told me that whenever he attended a medical meeting, he carried my medical case history in his briefcase. He was always ready to discuss my plight with whoever showed an active interest in lupus.

Listening to Dr. Gardner's footsteps fade down the hall, I felt grateful for his interest. He and the other doctors at Peter Bent Brigham Hospital seemed to combine knowledge with warmth and informality. I was privileged indeed to have such a share of their care and attention, and that was very important to me at this particular moment.

On my third day in the hospital, an old symptom recurred. The subcutaneous nodules under the extensor surface (outer side) of my elbow reappeared. They felt tender. Also, smaller nodules a little harder in texture than those showed clearly on my fingers. Now a doctor would surely see them before they vanished!

Several doctors examined the nodules. Their divided opinions echoed the confusion of my disease. One doctor thought that they were the same as those found in patients with rheumatoid arthritis; another agreed with him, but thought that in rheumatoid arthritis the nodules usually did not regress, as mine did, without medication. And a third declared that, in his opinion, these nodules definitely were a sign of systemic lupus, for in rheumatoid arthritis, the nodules did not regress at all, medicine or no medicine!

An hour later, a staff surgeon came in and sat at the edge of my bed. He carefully examined my elbows and fingers and detected some soft tissue swelling in my joints.

Half an hour later, a nurse wheeled me into the operating room and the same surgeon removed a tiny lump from the lower inner side of my left index finger. All I felt was the prick of the Novocaine needle.

The next morning the surgeon stopped by my door and reported briefly that the pathologist had found a mild inflammatory reaction but nothing more specific. "The biopsy was not interpreted as giving evidence of SLE," he said, and added, "If I were in your shoes, by now I would pack up and leave the place before they thought of other tests to do."

I told him that the thought had occurred to me more than once.

A couple of days later, Dr. Gardner told me that he had asked a lupus specialist whom I shall call Dr. Koenig, from California, to come see me. "He'll be in sometime this afternoon. We'll see what he has to say." Dr. Gardner, who always liked to explain things, added, "Dr. Koenig seems to think that patients with SLE could be helped by regular fresh white-blood-cell injections."[31]

"What do you mean by regular?" I asked.

"Twice a week—indefinitely—who knows?" he answered with a quizzical expression. "The rationale of the white-blood injections has not proved out conclusively."

"Do you have any idea how these injections work?"

"Not really. Dr. Koenig is basing his theory on the

premise that some enzyme causes damage to the DNA,*
and that normal white cells supply a missing factor
which inhibits the damage.

"DNA!" I was frequently amused by Dr. Gardner's
assumptions that I understood medical terminology as
well as all the members of his staff.

"DNA is a vital constituent of every cell. It is the
genetic substance, the identity of the cell," he
explained.

Dr. Koenig arrived that same afternoon. He walked
into my room with quick strides. Following him were
Dr. Thorn, Dr. Diamond, Dr. Gardner, and a large group
of interns and medical students. Dr. Koenig, a medium-
sized man with a very serious expression, examined me
with quick, nimble fingers. I observed his every motion,
wondering if he were aware that I was still a breathing
woman under the hospital covers.

"How do you feel?" he asked me with a friendly
look.

"Okay," I nodded.

"How is your appetite?"

"The cortisone makes me feel hungry all the time."

"Your patient looks good," he turned to Dr. Diamond who was standing closest to him.

"But she doesn't feel too well." Dr. Diamond, always
attentive, gave me a reassuring look. He turned to Dr.
Koenig. "Don't let her deceive you. She has pride."

One young student winked at me. I smiled back at
him. From the conversation at my bedside, I learned
that the Los Angeles County Hospital, an institute of
3500 beds, had an LE Research Laboratory. Several
thousands of LE cell preparations had been performed

---

*DNA: Deoxyribonucleic acid, a large complex molecule composed of
chemicals called sugars and nucleic acids.

there on many individuals in the past several years. Dr. Koenig also mentioned that in several other hospitals in the country LE cell tests were randomly performed on all patients in whom SLE or other rheumatoid diseases were suspected. At one point, Dr. Gardner interjected that, since he had started handling my case, he was tempted to perform the test on all women with diagnostic problems.

Dr. Koenig suggested a regimen of increased doses of cortisone plus 5 cc injections of fresh white blood cells twice a week. The latter treatment was very new and had not yet been used in Boston. The next day, Dr. Gardner prepared a fresh white cell concentrate in his laboratory and gave me the first of a long series of painful injections which were bearable only because I hoped for their success. A week later I went home with no fever but feeling sicker than ever.

The search for drugs was in the past a purely empirical venture. And, despite lofty attempts at a rational approach to this problem, its greatest achievements are still the result of chance or at best of trial and error.

—RENÉ DUBOS
Mirage of Health

NICOTINIC ACID

THE FRESH WHITE blood cells and cortisone did not produce the hoped-for effect. The clinical picture remained unchanged. After a few weeks of the increased dose of cortisone, ⊥ retained over ten pounds of fluid. Dr. Gardner prescribed acetazolamide (Diamox) as a diuretic. In about a week I developed a sore on my right arm—identical, it seemed to me, to the one I had developed on my leg in Sofia during my bout with erysipelas. I recalled again the miracle drug I had been given in Sofia and mentioned it to Dr. Gardner.

Without a word, he made a quarter turn in his chair, pulled a thick volume from the shelf on the left, and opened it on his desk. I detected a trace of excitement on his face as he finished reading. "I thought so!" he exclaimed. "The Diamox I gave you is chemically related to sulfonamide, and probably is capable of causing the same side effects. We'll have to change the drug. You must be terribly allergic to sulfonamides; very few people would have reacted to such a minimal dose. From now on, we must be absolutely sure of everything

71

you take. A drug sensitivity like yours will get us into trouble wherever we turn."

Was it possible that the sulfonamides did not just worsen my condition but had actually given me the disease? What a frightening thought. I looked up at Dr. Gardner and asked him if the sulfonamides had been available in the late thirties.

"Yes, they were," he said.

"I wonder . . ."

"You could be quite right." He guessed at my thoughts. "The 'miracle drug' you took in Bulgaria could very well have been a sulfonamide."

"What makes one person allergic to drugs and not another?"

"What makes one person susceptible to an infection and another immune?"* he echoed. "We know so little. We often learn by our mistakes." After some moments, he added, "Allergic people like you seem to do better on no drugs at all. Too often we overmedicate people for minor complaints. We should be more careful."

Terrible questions came to my mind, such as, had the "miracle drugs" in Bulgaria started my trouble? Had the sulfonamides given in Holland unmasked my condition for the second time? Were the doctors in Boston, however well-intentioned, giving me the wrong drugs to relieve my symptoms? Did the powder I applied to my rash contain sulfonamides? Did the medicated cream I applied to my sores contain sulfonamide? Were there other hidden routes by which sulfonamide could enter my body which even the doctors were not aware of?† [32]

God, there must be thousands of people all over the

---

*Immunity: The power to resist infection or invasion of bacteria.

†In February of 1972, an article in a Boston newspaper reported that over 100 billion meat animals and poultry had been routinely fed sulfonamide, penicillin, tetracycline, and other antibiotics during the past two decades.

place who react as I do. Or am I just one of the few unlucky ones who cannot take a very useful medicine?

Dr. Diamond had told me that penicillin and several other commonly used drugs could produce LE cells with similar systemic manifestations like mine.

Dr. Gardner was pensive, too.

"Dr. Gardner," I said, "suppose the sulfonamides are at the root of my problem, and what I have now is a type of lupus caused by sulfonamides—would that change the prognosis? Would I stand a better chance to get well?"

"It is reasonable to hope that everything will clear up if we remove the source of the trouble. It would be interesting," he mused, "to see how many other patients have the same problem.[33] It could shed light on the nature of lupus itself."

When I got up to leave, he asked, "By the way, how is your weight?"

"I am retaining lots of fluids, but I also must be gaining real weight. My appetite is uncontrollable. All of my clothes are too tight. This only adds to my depression."

"Cortisone does that," he said, getting up himself.

"Does what? Retains fluids or accentuates my problems?"

"It can do both."[34]

"So, now I can expect to lose my mind, too," I half smiled.

On my way out, Dr. Gardner said he was sorry he couldn't offer me anything for the moment to alleviate my problems—he could only sympathize with me. However, he assured me that, once we withdrew the cortisone, my weight would return to normal and my outlook would improve.[35]

Returning home that afternoon, I found Dr. and Mrs. Floyd Black waiting for me in my living room. How could I know that, for the second time in my life, these dear people would prove to be my saviors? I had known them since my youth in Bulgaria. Dr. Black had been the president of the American College in Sofia when I left home for the United States. He had helped me to obtain my American visa and was personally responsible for my being in this country. When he retired in 1955, he and his wife came to live in Arlington, Massachusetts.

Mrs. Black's keen eyes sensed my low spirit. "Poor girl," she said in her motherly voice. "You don't feel too well?"

"No, I don't," I admitted, on the verge of tears.

"I know that you don't like to talk about it, but what do you call this illness of yours?"

Dr. Black gave me a long look, then he removed his heavy-rimmed glasses to wipe them. For the first time in all these years I saw his eyes. They were a special blue, the color of water that had absorbed the sky.

"I feel like a hypochondriac whenever I talk about it," I mumbled.

"Poor girl," Mrs. Black repeated.

"The doctors believe that I have systemic lupus erythematosus. But they don't know much about the disease. They think it is incurable," I said, and started to cry.

"That's strange," Mrs. Black's voice quivered with feelings. "My nephew had systemic lupus erythematosus in Bulgaria more than thirty years ago."

I wiped my eyes and looked at her in surprise. She was the first person outside the medical profession whom I had heard pronounce correctly and without hesitation the words "lupus erythematosus." This was the first time that I'd heard of someone who had actually had lupus.

Dr. Black confirmed her statement. He said that Jordan, their nephew, had been working for the

American College of Sofia when he was stricken with lupus. Today, he was still healthy and sound. "He lives practically next door to you, right here in Wellesley," Dr. Black said with an encouraging smile.

"You should call Jordan up this very evening," Mrs. Black urged excitedly. "His sister who is a doctor in Sofia treated his lupus with some simple medication and he got well!"

"At least well enough not to have mentioned lupus for more than thirty years." Dr. Black glanced at me with one of his mischievous expressions.

I wanted so much to believe that they were not in error. My doctors in Boston had no records of any lupus patient who had survived for such a long period of time. Still, I had to explore every possible clue. Immediately after supper, I telephoned Jordan. The Blacks had already alerted him and he volunteered to come to our house for a cup of coffee.

That evening when Jordan, sturdy and well, walked into our living room, I tried to hide my excitement. His dark complexion and heavy accent made him appear to the children as a true Bulgarian. Martha was somewhat disappointed that the nephew was so old. He was at least fifty. To her, someone's nephew had to be closer to her own age.

Jordan was reluctant to speak of his illness. Only after he understood my predicament did he open up. We began to compare notes. Most of the symptoms I mentioned, he had also experienced; only in his opinion, his ordeal had been worse than mine. Through the evening, Jordan confessed that at one point his suffering had reached such a degree that he believed death to be his only salvation. I knew then that his case must have been graver than mine.

Jordan said that in 1937 he had gone to Geneva

where the doctors diagnosed lupus from a biopsy* from his cheek. He pointed to a faint scar under his left eye. His sister, who had been working at the same hospital, had cared for him. Once the doctors had established the diagnosis, she began to treat him on the advice of her colleagues in Sofia with a simple medication which brought about a remission. Whenever he anticipated a slight relapse, he fell back on the same medication, and all went well again.

I listened to Jordan with a strange feeling of suspense. I mentioned that I had understood from the Blacks that he had had the disease during the German occupation of Bulgaria in 1941.

"I had it then, too," Jordan said and explained that living conditions were trying during those times, and may have had something to do with causing the relapse of many diseases, lupus included. His relapse had lasted for many months, but he had been well ever since. I was eager to hear the name of this remarkable medication. At that point, I was willing to accept witchcraft if witchcraft would help me.

"What's the name of the medication?" my husband asked seconds before I did.

"Nicotinamide,"[36] Jordan said. "The drug is frequently referred to as niacin; it's one of the B complex vitamins. It's more commonly known as a preventive medication for pellagra.† That's what saved my life!" he nodded with obvious pleasure.

"Can one take niacin pills?" I asked, tempted already to rush to the drugstore and buy the magic drug as soon as Jordan left the house.

"It's possible," Jordan said, "but one gets better

---

*Biopsy: A sample of tissue for microscopic study.
†Pellagra: A deficiency of niacin, one of the B vitamins, which causes diarrhea, dermatitis, and dementia.

results if he takes it intravenously. You can take it also by injection into the muscle."

He suggested that I write to his sister, a physician in Bulgaria, to find out more details of his medical history. He thought that Dr. Gardner might find it of value to know if his condition were clinically similar to mine. "If Bulgaria were free," he said, "I'd advise you to go to Sofia to see Professor Liuben Popoff. He is a well-known dermatologist. The doctors might know of him at Peter Bent Brigham," Jordan speculated. "Professor Popoff is among the first to have used the antimalarial drugs successfully in rheumatoid arthritis and lupus." And, half-kiddingly, while bidding us good night, he suggested once more that perhaps I should take the trip to Bulgaria.

"Go to Bulgaria?" my husband mumbled after Jordan was gone. "How can one go to Bulgaria? The State Department won't grant protection to any United States citizen who wants to go there. Even if the new Bulgarian government would let someone in, there would be no guarantee they'd let him out again."

I lay down on the couch and closed my eyes. . . . The nicotinic acid grew in my mind as a symbol of new life. . . . A trip to Bulgaria! All my emotions churned. Homesickness and sadness merged into pain. Nostalgic echoes from the past came back to mind. Surrendering completely, I fell to dreaming. As a growing girl, I had often seen myself traveling and exploring the world with curiosity. Now, I was in America thousands of miles from home and I suddenly longed to be back in my parents' house.

I remembered the last morning at home. From our kitchen window, the snowdrops and the jonquils seemed saturated with sunshine. The flowers in our backyard expanded into fields of wild daisies that led to the pine woods and to the mountains where I used to spend every

free minute of my life. I could almost hear the gushing
springs breaking through the ice with thundering noises
that echoed through the valley. Coming down the slopes
on skiis chased by the spring winds felt like flying into
space. At night the stars hung low, almost within reach.
I was tempted to pluck them for sheer pleasure but
never had. I'd always left them there for the next
time.

I could see Mother reading by the window in her low,
cushioned chair. I had always suspected that besides the
light, she'd chosen the window because of its closeness
to the street. There, the outside world began—the
people walking, the children playing. To Mother, the
world was an extension of her home.

I was cold, but I closed my eyes a little tighter, afraid
that I would break the spell. I could see the train pulling
out of the Sofia railroad station; that evening Mother's
eyes looked like emeralds, only greener. They shone like
stars bathed in tears. As I watched her, I knew I would
never again see eyes so wise, so human, and so tender,
for they were Mother's eyes; in them I clearly saw her
soul and all her love for me.

German soldiers, their uniforms ornate with glowing
yellow brass, packed the station, darker and more
desolate than usual. The rhythmic clicking of the
soldiers' spurs and the piercing whistle of the steam
engine still reverberate in my mind. The air that night
was heavily charged with fear and anticipation of
impending disaster. The Germans had been in the
country only for a few hours. I could not adjust to
seeing so many young men carrying guns and pistols,
objects reflecting hatred and savagery. The cold, icy
expressions on their soldier faces drained of humor and
passion, even of cruelty, made them seem like phantoms
walking in the semidarkness. The only civilians on the
platform were Mother and Father and a few friends and

relatives who had come to see me off. In a way we
looked like phantoms, too.

Father rushed to get me on the train. He walked with
me from one compartment to another looking for a
seat. I was the only girl on that train—the rest were
German soldiers. Eventually, he found a place next to
an open window, embraced me, and rushed out.

When Mother saw me, her voice trembled like a leaf.
"Don't be . . ." the whistle's piercing sound muffled the
rest of her words. The train gave a jolt, another whistle,
and we were moving. Father found the strength to joke
in those inhuman moments, hoping to bring a smile to
my face. "Don't forget," he called out loudly, trying to
keep up with the train that gathered speed. "Act like a
boy scout; forget that you are just a girl."

What a fantastic trip that turned out to be. To get to
America from Bulgaria, I had to travel over the Black
Sea to Russia, cross the whole of Siberia to the Yellow
Sea, to Japan, and over the Pacific to San Francisco.

In the past few days a letter had arrived from my
brother. He reminded me that we had inherited from
our parents good health. "Mother handed us her perse-
verance and Father his imagination. . . ." He compared
them to technology and the humanities. . . .

My thoughts were derailed as my husband threw a
blanket over me. "You seem to be shivering." He looked
at me with a strange glance.

"I am always cold," I whispered, trying to conceal
my tears.

In bed, after he put the lights out, he said, "Perhaps
you should go to Geneva and see some of Jordan's Swiss
doctors. They might have a different approach to your
problems. Often the methods of treating disease differ
from place to place and the details are not known
everywhere at the same time. The change might do you
some good."

Long after he fell asleep, I lay there thinking. I could not risk going to Bulgaria in my condition. What if they kept me there? I tossed, restless, unable to fall asleep. Go to Geneva?

During my next appointment with Dr. Gardner, I related Jordan's story of the nicotinic acid. I asked him if he would mind writing to Jordan's sister. He said that he didn't mind writing but was skeptical of the nicotinic acid. He knew the drug to be useful in the treatment of pellagra, but whether or not it might have any effect on lupus, he didn't know. After some reflection, Dr. Gardner said, "I will give you the nicotinic acid injections if you want me to. . . ." I could follow his thoughts: 'A placebo* has proved helpful in other diseases,[37] so why not try a placebo in this one?"

"I want to have the injections," I said.

"All right," he said, "but to treat you with nicotinic acid would be the same as closing my eyes and, from a shelf full of harmless potions, taking out just anything and giving it to you." Drawing a memo pad from the right top pocket of his white coat, he wrote down "nicotinic acid," saying that this wouldn't be the first time he had made a fool of himself by experimenting. He put the pad back into his lab-coat pocket which seemed to contain everything: pencils, pens, slide rule. . . .On occasion I had seen there tubes full of blood and once he had managed to squeeze in a small plastic bag of plasma† that looked like a fresh liver. "I'll do some inquiring about the nicotinic acid," he said, "but I'll only buy the idea when I have some clinical proof." He handed me a prescription for hydroxy-chloroquine, saying that some patients with lupus had

---

*Placebo: An inactive substance given to patient either for its pleasing effect or as a control in experiments with an active drug.

†Plasma: The fluid portion of the blood in which the blood cells are floating.

responded favorably to it. He'd wanted to give it a try, but he was candid enough to stress that he really hadn't found a positive LE cell in my blood.

The hydroxychloroquine was supposed to reduce the light sensitivity of the skin. Its ability to do this had, in common with many other medical discoveries, been found by accident. The drug is one of a group of malaria-control medicines which were first used on a large scale by the United States Armed Forces in the Pacific theater during World War II. Some very alert physicians noticed that discoid lupus cases seemed to benefit from the malaria prophylaxis. It was then reasoned that if discoid LE could be helped, perhaps the systemic LE would also be benefited by the same family of drugs. Dr. Gardner felt that hydroxychloroquine produced the least side effects* of the entire group.

"What kind of side effects?" I asked.

He said that visual changes had been reported in patients on prolonged chloroquin therapy.[38] This meant that while on the medication, I had to be checked periodically by an eye specialist. "It would be wise," he cautioned, "to take the medicine intermittently. Let's say, take it for four months—then rest for a few. You should take it during the summer months when the sun is at its strongest." I asked if the eye examination would provide absolute assurance of safety.

He said, "No," but I should not worry about it because the dose I was about to take was probably not large enough to pose any problems. But one could never be sure. All sorts of problems, minor and major, had been reported with this drug. Every drug has the ability to hurt someone. "But don't worry. Don't think about

---

*Side effect: An adverse effect produced by a drug. One disorder is being replaced by another.

it, otherwise you and I will be paralyzed and won't be able to do anything."

During the discussion about hydroxychloroquine, I had made up my mind. I told Dr. Gardner that I had just decided to take a trip to Geneva.

"I follow your thinking," Dr. Gardner said. "You want to see for yourself. Actually, I myself am rather curious about the nicotinic acid. My only concern is over the possibility of your getting fatigued by the journey. But on the other hand the change might do you some good."

Traveling had always satisfied a need for adventure in me and I was glad the feeling had not diminished with my illness. Besides, I had to find out all I could about the nicotinic acid. I seized upon the drug as a thread of hope.

Dr. Gardner gave me a white-cell injection which made a tetanus shot seem like a tea party. First came the burning, then a predictable soreness and swelling the size of a lemon which lasted until it was time for the next injection the following week. With the injection completed, he seemed to notice my pained reaction to it, and, trying to cheer me up, he said he would try the nicotinic acid as soon as I returned from Geneva.

Before I changed my mind about taking the trip, I asked him to give me the smallpox vaccination required by immigration law. Then I remembered Dr. Koenig's visit. I had gained the impression that something drastic might occur if I stopped taking the white-cell injections. When I expressed my worries to Dr. Gardner, he said that he had been planning to talk to Dr. Koenig about the possibility of stopping the shots. I had already had over one hundred such injections and he didn't think they were helping much. And besides, he was concerned that I might get hepatitis. He explained that the type of hepatitis that concerned him was a disease transmitted by human-blood products. If even one drop of plasma from a hepatitis carrier entered the bloodstream, the recipient could contract the disease. "The chance of getting hepatitis from one hundred blood donors sounds like Russian roulette, doesn't it?" Then he gave me the smallpox inoculations.

Two days after I had the smallpox inoculation, a terrific reaction set in. My arm swelled up. An angry sore erupted, raging like a volcano full of pus. My temperature rose to 101 degrees. For a few days it appeared as if I might have to cancel my trip. Dr. Gardner wondered whether the immunization had stirred up a new allergy. Other types of inoculations had been known to cause problems with lupus.[39] Fortunately, the sore improved after a week and I was able to go ahead with my plans.

Not sure that I could withstand the flight, I took a night plane with sleeping accommodations to London. From there, I flew to Geneva, where I was met by Madeleine and Noel Landru, close friends of ours who live in Voiron, France, forty miles over the border. They had reserved a room for me at a hotel in the center of town and suggested that I stay there for a day or so until I entered the hospital. I told them I would keep the room through my stay in Geneva. We made plans to drive out together to Chamonix in southeastern France for a ten-day holiday after my release from the hospital.

HOSPITAL IN GENEVA

ON MAY 29, 1959, I entered one of the largest hospitals in Geneva, the same one that Jordan had stayed in thirty years before. The price per day was thirty-six Swiss francs, slightly under nine dollars. I was asked by the cashier to make a deposit of 650 francs, "for all eventualities." He seemed disturbed that I had no one in Switzerland to be notified in case of death, and offered to notify a church of my choice. On the entry blank I had to write my maiden name, married name, number of children, their ages and sexes, my occupation, place of birth, date of birth, nationality, passport number, place of issue, and religion. I was given a number, 4673/11, and from then on I was referred to by this number. When I inquired of Jordan's doctor, I was told that the man was gravely ill and hospitalized himself—an unfortunate situation, as he had been the reason for my trip.

A broad-bosomed nurse who spoke perfect English fetched me into the cashier's office. She didn't walk like a woman or even like a man, but more like a bird, hopping with incredible speed. I followed her as best I could to the elevator, up to the second floor, to a small private room with a high ceiling and two narrow windows showing a quiet street of gray-stone houses.

The nurse told me to undress, showed me where to hang my clothes, and asked me to empty my bladder in a white enamel bedpan. She stuck a thermometer in my mouth and left the room. She returned almost immediately with a syringe and several glass tubes. I expected her to insert the needle painfully, but she was deft and I didn't feel it.

Shortly, a doctor whom I shall call Professor de Malraux walked in. With him came a young female assistant. Her eyes were in constant motion, like round black beets shaken in a jar. The professor spoke only French, but his assistant spoke English with a thick, nasal French accent. Another young doctor walked in. He was of a ruddy complexion with light blond hair and extremely polite. I noticed when he bumped into the corner of my bed, he apologized in the most courteous way.

Professor de Malraux knew Jordan and Jordan's sister well, though he remembered only vaguely the details of Jordan's illness. He seemed astounded that I had come to consult doctors in Geneva when the United States—Boston in particular—was considered at the time the outstanding center of medicine in the world. When I explained my interest in the nicotinic acid, I was sure he knew what I was talking about, but he chose not to acknowledge it. Such simple medications were out of the question when more modern drugs like cortisone were available, he said, and that was that.

The spirit of this hospital proved very different from that of Peter Bent Brigham. The countenances were stern, especially the nurses—their starched expressions matched their crisp uniforms. In the presence of the doctors those women stood at attention like soldiers before their generals. At periodic intervals they took my blood pressure, pulse, and temperature, and I was fed at regular hours. There was a coldness in this hospital that separated the staff from the patients and one another. There was no friendliness.

Professor de Malraux moved in and out of my room, glowing in power like a celestial body. Not once did he tell me what tests were being taken. I didn't know from one moment to the next what to expect; everything kept me on edge.

On the second morning, a tall doctor with narrow stooped shoulders came to examine my eyes. He had a large head and a very dour expression. Whenever his droopy cheek touched mine, I cringed. He spoke curtly, telling me in which direction to focus and nothing else. At the end of the examination, which lasted for over half an hour, he put several drops in each eye and left without a word. Later, when I opened my eyes, I was practically blind. The room, pitch black, moved in circles, spun by my exaggerated fear. Gradually, a blurred vision reappeared. For the next few hours, I kept checking my eyes, anxiously trying to read my illustrated magazine. I was tense and fearful that the damage would be permanent. That night I couldn't fall asleep.

The next day, when a nurse wheeled me in for a cardiogram, the doctor, a stocky muscular man, studied the strips of paper from the machine in perfect silence. When he was finished, I asked him if the electrocardiogram was all right.

He looked up in surprise and murmured a few incomprehensible words, and before I had a chance to say anything more, he stuck the strips of paper in his pocket, turned his back indifferently, and left the room.

The nurse who wheeled me back spoke only in a Romansh dialect, which bore no resemblance to any other language I'd ever heard. I learned later that most of the nurses and attendants at this hospital had been recruited from the Romansh-speaking area of Switzerland.

Finally, the four days at the hospital mercifully came to an end. Professor de Malraux walked in with his young, pale blond assistant. He declared that all the tests were concluded. No LE cell had been found—nothing suggestive of systemic lupus erythematosus. In his opinion, even the faded rash on my face was not a typical LE rash. He had seen such rashes before caused by drugs.[40] When his young assistant pointed to the red V on my neck, Professor de Malraux impatiently muttered, "Yes, yes, drugs can cause the redness on the neck like hers. It can involve the cheeks, the nose, the brow," he made a motion with his hand over the bridge of his nose. Then he turned to me again. "If your rash grows redder again, apply some Ichthyol."

"Calamine lotion is close enough," murmured his assistant with a wisp of a polite smile.

"The persistent leukopenia could have been induced by drugs, too," Professor de Malraux addressed his assistant. I wondered what he meant by drugs. What kind of drugs? I remembered once having taken tetracycline* for an infected sore throat. The doctors in Boston had not been sure at the time that the drug had helped my throat, but had rejoiced that at least I could tolerate an antibiotic. Two months later, when I had contracted a bladder infection and the "cranberry juice" cure didn't work, I took tetracycline again. This time, after only three tablets, my temperature soared to 102 degrees, a rash erupted over my entire body, I had chills, and my eyes swelled up. I wished I could ask Professor de Malraux what he meant by "stay away from drugs," but he spoke much too fast. I could hardly understand what he was saying. I am sure I had spoken better French before my admission to this hospital. Once inside, the language failed me and I was sure the unfriendly atmosphere had something to do with the problem.

---

*Tetracycline: An antibiotic effective against many of the bacteria which are not affected by penicillin.

"Madame, you will be all right." Professor de Malraux forced a smile while his eyes remained as hard as marbles. "You must be careful not to become a chronic complainer. . . ."

A flash of indignation rushed all my blood to my cheeks. Here I was lying in bed feeling like a deflated balloon, even too weak to speak. Was he implying that my pains and aches were psychoneurotic? Was I turning into a hypochondriac?

Impervious to my emotions, Professor de Malraux said that he was intrigued by the white-blood-cell injections I had mentioned to him before. He had written already to Boston for more information. He said he would send the report of my visit to Dr. Gardner at Peter Bent Brigham Hospital. For the first time he recalled having met Dr. George Thorn at a medical meeting in Belgium. His voice bordered on reverence when he pronounced Dr. Thorn's name.

While Professor de Malraux spoke, his assistant was eying the eruption on my arm caused by the smallpox inoculation. Cautiously, he expressed some concern over the inflammation, saying obliquely that perhaps I should not have been vaccinated. Both men bent down to examine the sore more closely, but neither said a word. Not be vaccinated? How, I thought, could he expect me to return home without it?

Professor de Malraux wished me a good trip back to the States. His assistant remained in my room for another few moments. He handed me a tiny booklet which described the effects of the sun on the skin throughout the year and the intensity of the ultraviolet rays at different times of the day. He also gave me a prescription for Niconacid,* 0.05, to be taken morning,

---

*Niconacid: Swiss-French trademark for a preparation of nicotinic acid.

noon, and evening, and another prescription for a salve, called Homel creme, to rub on my face daily. He explained that the salve would shield me from the sun. He warned me that in my case the sun could be most troublesome.

Dangers, real or imaginary, crept deeper into my subconscious. I left the hospital in the worst possible mood. That night I spent tossing and turning, unable to sleep. I felt depressed and angry with myself for having taken this idiotic trip. But, then again, I reasoned, I could not go against my nature. I could not leave any stone unturned. Suppose some truth resided in the nicotinic acid, suppose my trip had revealed more about the drug. I recalled again the story of the chloroquine, which, since 1941, had been used successfully in the treatment of lupus in Bulgaria and other parts of Europe, yet had not been used in the United States until much later. The same transatlantic route of acceptance might well be true of nicotinic acid. At least I hoped so.

When morning came, I was still awake. I wanted to be fresh and rested when my friends appeared the next evening, so that afternoon I asked the pharmacist in the apothecary next to the hotel for a mild sedative. I explained very clearly that I was sensitive to drugs, all drugs, and had never before taken a sleeping pill. The man behind the counter instantly handed me a tiny box. "*One* pill will put you to sleep, madame," he nodded amiably. "You'll sleep like a child."

After supper, while I packed my bags, I took two pills to insure sleep. That's all I remember until I was awakened by the shrill ring of the telephone. I found myself fully dressed, shoes and all, sprawled on the bed. I could not imagine what had happened. Madeleine Landru was calling from the lobby. Sensing my confusion, she asked if I felt all right.

"Yes, I am fine, fine," I repeated. Groggily, I mentioned the sleeping pills I had taken at nine that night.

"Nine?" Madeleine repeated in a curious tone. "Then you have slept for twenty-two hours. It is seven-ten now!"

"Seven-ten?" I quickly glanced at the red traveling clock on my night table. "What day of the week is it?" I asked, as I began to realize what must have happened. Next, I heard a pounding on my door.

"C'est moi. Tu m'écoute?" I heard Madeleine's voice from afar. I had dozed off again, dreaming the most fantastic dream.

Madeleine helped me finish packing. "Some pills!" I remarked. I was frightened to think that I had lost an entire day.

"You must be terribly sensitive to drugs," Madeleine said.

I answered her with a drowsy yawn. An hour later we left Geneva and I slept in the Landrus' car through the border inspection and all.

We spent the night in Voiron, and set out for Chamonix the following morning. As Noel drove along the narrow winding mountain roads, my short dream of two nights before returned vividly to my mind. Death in the abstract has always interested me in a philosophical way, and the end of life has filled me with curiosity. In my dream I had experienced the point of death. I had seen myself lying in bed at home, flat on my back, both arms stretched down by my side, my head tilted slightly to the left. My eyes were closed or possibly open just a slit. By my bedside my husband, son, and two daughters sat in contemplation. Their faces seemed sad and withdrawn, but did I actually see them or just imagine that I did? I was absolutely sure that these were my last moments. I had no power left over my body. The sensation reminded me of the time in Holland at the onset of my disease when I had awakened in the middle of the night with no sensation in my arms. But in the dream I felt no fear at all. I was not fighting death; I was at peace with myself. My consciousness was slipping away; already my brain functioned in a limited fashion. My world was shrinking to the row of chairs where my family sat; everything else was forgotten or didn't matter anymore. I felt their emotions keenly. In time I knew my husband would overcome his sorrow. My son, too, would manage somehow, and so would my oldest daughter. But Martha—she needed to be reassured that I felt at peace. In time of stress, we had a special signal between us; I used to smile at her a certain way to tell her not to worry. Just before my dream ended, a rush of warmth touched my lips and I knew that Martha had gotten the message.

The dream cast a gloomy spell on me. I had tried to be as little of a worry to my family as possible, but how could they not be affected by my illness? Now that I was away, I could perceive more deeply their suppressed fears, their constant worry. I felt guilty and sorry for them. What could I do to lessen their burden? I still believed that some day I'd get well. As images from the dream kept reemerging, my thoughts returned to the act of dying, and death itself. I questioned if I had the strength to give up all the things I loved. "I'll miss the smell of freshly cut grass . . ." I whispered to myself, "the feel of damp soil squeezed between my fingers; the spring, the summer, the fall, the winter . . ." I remembered a poem by Loren Eiseley I'd read some months before Some of the lines resounded in my mind:

> *I shall be part of all Octobers*
> *I shall be part of sleet and driving rain,*
> *I shall scurry with dead leaves on pavements,*
> *I shall be dust and rise from dust again.*[41]

I shuffled in my seat and Madeleine asked, "*Ça va?*"

"Yes, yes," I nodded to reassure her. But when I tried to stretch my legs, my knees felt locked; the pain was more than I could bear.

Noel drove fast with the skill of a magician. Except for a brief stop for lunch, we drove for eight hours from Voiron through to Chamonix. In places the narrow mountain roads clung to the edges of precipices that, from the car window, appeared dark and endless. I had the uncanny feeling of driving on a tightrope. By five in the afternoon, Noel had parked his Citroen in front of Hotel Mont Blanc in the center of Chamonix.

I stepped out with some difficulties. The aching and heaviness of my limbs had increased from having sat in the same position for so many hours. The crisp air made me shiver with cold. While Noel and Madeleine unloaded the car, I watched Mont Blanc. It looked like the Snow Queen bathed in the last rays of sunshine. Flowery bushes and trees covered the lower part of this giant beauty that towered nearly 16,000 feet over Europe. The top, covered by ice and snow, sparkled like precious stones. I followed a large white cumulus which drifted across the sky toward the ridges, and thought of the mountains back home in Sofia.

Noel had finished unloading the bags and now was standing by my side viewing the mountains. I saw him as young, the way he used to look when I knew him in Bulgaria. He, my husband, and I used to go skiing or hiking on Vitosha Mountain before I was married. Noel used to tease me about going too fast for him.

"The mountains never change, Noel," I said.

He glanced at me and in a flash of optimism said, "You'll see, everything will be all right."

After a good night's sleep with the help of aspirins, I dressed and went for a walk around the lodge. Completely surrendering to the beauty around me, I fell into one of my old mountain moods, which meant a relapse into childhood. I even tried to whistle again the way I used to in the mountains. No sound came; I had no strength to blow the air. My tired body could not keep up with my spirit. Since my arrival in Chamonix, I was aware my voice had faded some. During the day I could hardly talk. I began wondering if some day my voice would disappear altogether.

All my life I had loved to whistle, and the loss added to my misery. As a child this enthusiasm had often caused me trouble, for in Bulgaria girls were not supposed to whistle. But I always did. Whenever I came home from school, Mother would hear me whistling long before I reached the house, and she would reprimand me, "Girls don't whistle!" Minutes later I would have forgotten and started a new tune. I used to tease the birds in our garden for hours, imitating their songs. That irked not just Mother but some of the birds as well.

> But there is also an ecology of the
> world within our body. . . .
> —RACHEL CARSON
> *Silent Spring*

THE MAN WHO CARRIED THE MOUNTAINS IN HIS CHEST

TOWARD THE END of our stay in Chamonix, I rose very early one morning and went out of the hotel before the sun grew too hot. I was anxious to see the new tunnel being built under Mont Blanc. The entrance to the place did not look very spectacular, just a dark hole. But I was excited. The tunnel was destined to open a direct motor route between Chamonix and Italy, thus shortening the distance by many miles. How unbelievable, I thought, that men should have cracked open the tallest mountain of Europe to build an ultra-modern thoroughfare for thousands of cars. I searched around for someone to give me information about the project.

The small structure by the wire gate near the tunnel was deserted. Disappointed, I turned around to return to the hotel. And then I saw a man sitting on a large stone near me. His withered face and faded big blue eyes blended with the landscape. His arms were crossed over his chest the way as a child I was forced to sit in the French school in Bulgaria. The memory diverted me for a moment.

"*Les mains croisées et la bouche fermé,*" Sister

94

Celeste would chant the moment she entered the classroom. Both requests were torture for me. I could never sit still for more than a moment.

Close by, I saw the man was ashen in the sunlight. He watched me, too. My long-sleeved blouse, wide-brimmed hat, and the huge flowery unbrella, a gift from Madeleine to protect me from the sun, must have intrigued him. I asked him how I might have a glimpse of the tunnel. He unfolded his arms with the air of a martyr. After he cleared his throat several times, he muttered that women were not allowed in the hellish place. Between wheezes and coughs, he added that even men could visit only on official business. "Why do you want to see the damn place?" he hissed unexpectedly.

"Just curious," I gave him a quick look and started to move away.

"*Attendez*," he called after me, "I can tell you all you want to know about the tunnel."

Something in his voice made me stop. "When will the tunnel be opened?" I asked, noticing his eyes again. They looked like blue pools full of sorrow.

He shook his head. "Who knows? It might take them another six months, maybe a year, but I won't live long enough to see this work of evil finished. I won't last through the fall." I looked at him aghast.

"It's a dump, madame, fit only for the devil to work in," he breathed with his mouth open. "For two and a half years I've swallowed dust and granite in that hole. My saliva mudballed in my mouth while I blasted the blasted granite." A fit of coughing that seemed to tear his chest apart interrupted him.

"You are a pessimist, monsieur," I said, by now breathing as rapidly as he was. "People don't die just like that."

He glanced at the tunnel with hatred. His breathing sounded like nothing I had ever heard before. Then he relaxed some and explained that conditions on this project were much improved over what they used to be in other places. He was one of the few casualties on this job. "*Les pauvres chrétiens*," he muttered. "They used to die like flies from silicosis, just like me."

"I've never heard of silicosis."

"*Tiens!*" He uttered. "You've never heard of silicosis?"

"No, I've never heard of it." We were beginning to share a feeling of intimacy.

"It's a lung disease, madame," he tapped his chest with his thumb. "The doctor calls it an occupational sickness. It comes from blasting quartz, it's pure silica. I was told that the dust causes a fibrosis of the lung tissue. The disease spreads, madame, it spreads like fire; my lungs have decayed. . . ."

"What do you do for your silicosis?"

His lips twisted. "When the disease has spread like mine, one can do nothing. Perhaps, if the blasted thing is discovered in time, one could survive. But how is one to know? Everyone down there coughs." With that he was swept by a new outburst of coughing. "*Tiens!*" he repeated and gasped for air. "You've never heard of silicosis!"

"No, I've never heard of silicosis," I said, "but I know how you must feel. I have lupus. My condition is incurable, too." I guessed by his expression that he hadn't heard of lupus, either.

"*Tiens,*" he shook his head a little. "I've never heard of . . ."

"Lupus, systemic lupus."

"*Tiens,*" he repeated, then asked if I had any other questions about the damn tunnel.

"I've lost my interest in the damn place." The word "damn" made him laugh. Then he lapsed into a new coughing spell. I could almost hear the pieces of

mountain rattling in his lungs. When his chest relaxed, I
gave him my hand. I thought he kept it for a moment
longer in his cold bony fingers. We looked at each other,
he with his hopeless occupational disease, and I with a
disease that I suspected had been made worse by
medical progress.

I walked toward the path that led downhill to Hotel
Mont Blanc. The strange stillness of the valley grew
stiller. Before I turned the last corner, I looked back at
him once more. He appeared tiny now, almost a part of
the stone.

The holiday in Chamonix helped me improve my
spirit. The day before departure I remembered the
prescriptions given to me by Professor de Malraux's
assistant in Geneva and stopped by a pharmacy to buy
them. I asked the pharmacist what the pills were for and
he said, "Nicotinic acid helps. It helps pellagra and other
photosensitive diseases. The other prescription, the
cream, is also good. It will protect you from the sun." I
could have kissed him. He almost made my trip to
Geneva worthwhile.

The Landrus drove me back to Geneva from where I
was to take a plane to Paris. The long ride drained all
my strength again. I was sure I was running a fever, but I
refused to check it. I dreaded the thought of being
hospitalized again away from home.

I felt exhausted when I arrived in Paris—my head
ached and I had chills. From the airport I went straight
to the Hotel Louvois where I had previously stayed
several times. The staff never changed and they were all
charming people. When I entered the lobby, Jacques,
concierge, welcomed me warmly. Marie, the old cham-
bermaid, was still there. I saw her polishing a rail of
brass on the elevator and went to shake her hand. I told
her that the last time I had seen her, two years ago, she
had been polishing the same rail.

"You are probably right, madame," she nodded with amusement. Her narrow shrewd eyes noticed immediately that I wasn't feeling well. She told me she would come to give me a hand with the unpacking.

I knew that at the Louvois, if worse came to worst, I would be taken care of better than at any hospital in Paris. The hotel provided a haven of quiet and peace. I had a nicely furnished room—it looked onto the Square Louvois, a small park with a few ancient trees that smelled of eternity, even from a distance. The benches beneath the trees were old and weatherbeaten, the same color as the drab gray wall of La Bibliothèque Nationale, which I could see in the distance.

Since I had a fever and hence was confined to my room for a week, the Square Louvois became my world. The elderly people who came each day to sit in the park were always the same. A short plump woman with thick white hair appeared each morning wrapped in a heavy black woolen shawl to feed the birds. She carried the bird feed in a motley, quilted handbag. The woman, as she settled herself comfortably on the bench, spoke intimately to the birds while they chirped and fluttered with all the animation of sophisticated Parisians. Why would anyone talk to birds? I wondered. Perhaps she was lonely, I speculated. Perhaps the birds did not intimidate her. I remembered a friend of mine in Cambridge with whom I used to work at Widener Library at Harvard. She used to do the Sanscrit cataloging; I helped in the Slavic Department. After my friend retired from the library, occasionally I would see her walking around Harvard Square with a little bird perched on her shoulder. She never stuttered while speaking to her bird, though she did quite often when talking to one of her own species. "Perhaps the birds do not intimidate her," I told myself. I had never talked to myself before, but now I did. Watching the woman in the park, I recognized a likeness in us, however different we might be. I had been terribly lonely for the past week and I, too, felt a need to communicate.

In the evenings before I went to sleep, I sat on the balcony. People came like shadows to the Park Louvois. These weatherbeaten benches, I reflected, must know more stories of the human heart than all the books stocked on the shelves behind the gray wall of the Bibliothèque Nationale.

While I stayed at the Louvois, I could hardly eat any solid food. I was glad they cooked fresh *potage aux légume* every day. It helped to settle my stomach, which was in a state of upheaval from taking an arsenal of drugs.

It was most embarrassing to open my suitcases for the customs officials. Usually I put my pills right on top of everything else to get them over with as quickly as possible. I'd tell the inspector, "These are my medicines." I dreaded the moment. By now I was taking cortisone, chloroquine, potassium chloride, Serpasil, atropine, the nicotinic acid I bought in Chamonix, Pyribenzamine, and a row of vitamins—B_6, ascorbic acid, folic acid, riboflavin, and cod-liver oil concentrate.

On my last night in Paris I phoned my family in Wellesley to give my husband my flight numbers from Paris to London and from London to Boston. I told the children they could expect me at Logan Airport the following day at twelve o'clock Boston time. I could hardly wait to reach home.

The week I spent at the Louvois had been free of household duties and cares, and the rest had helped me to restore some energy for my flight back home. The next morning, I felt well enough to get up and have a cup of hot chocolate with Jacques in the lobby. He drove me to Orly. He was afraid I wouldn't make it by myself. He had watched me all these days walk through the hotel lobby, resting from time to time for breath. We arrived at the airport with an hour and a quarter to spare. The weather was fine; the brand-new Caravelle was moderately crowded. The seat next to mine was empty, and I looked forward to the luxury of a smooth flight and stretching out for an hour, just relaxing.

We taxied out. The twin engine aircraft almost cleared the runway. But straining for lift-off, it skidded across a stretch of field. The plane rattled convulsively like a giant bird trying to fly with broken wings. The pilot's voice crackled over the loudspeaker: "*Restez calme, s'il vous plait. Bitte bleiben Sie ruhig. Rimanete calmi.* . . . Please remain calm." No one stirred anyway. We were breathless. As the disturbance grew more violent, I smelled smoke and I braced myself for an explosion. After some endless minutes, the plane was brought to a standstill and a speedy evacuation was ordered. The police came right away. Sirens wailed as emergency equipment and Red Cross ambulances rushed to our assistance. Minibuses also converged to carry the passengers back to the terminal. Shaking, we praised the captain for averting a catastrophe, thankful to be safe after the near tragedy.

Of course, I had missed my London connection. An Air France officer informed me, however, that I was being transferred to an Air France jet due to leave in ten minutes for New York. They were already singling out my luggage from the damaged plane. I told him that I had to cable home. But he said that my luggage might not be found in time, and I could miss the new flight. Politely, he took my husband's name and address and promised, once I was safely on my way, to send the cable himself. My luggage came, and as I boarded the plane, he reassured me again about the cable and wished me *bon voyage.*

No cable reached home. When I didn't arrive at

Logan, my husband and children were frantic. They told me later they had called the Louvois and Jacques told my husband that he himself had seen me off at Orly. "It happens all the time, monsieur. Women are privileged to change their minds!" he added before he put down the receiver. But this light touch failed to abate my husband's anxiety. Next, he called London Airport, where he was told mistakenly that the Caravelle from Orly had arrived on schedule, but I was not among the passengers! At that point my husband felt sure I must have collapsed at the airport in Paris. Sensing his distress, the Englishman volunteered to call him back after he had done some checking.

Upon arrival in New York, I called home from Kennedy Airport, but there was no answer. I suspected that Air France had not notified my family of my landing in New York instead of Boston. I paged my husband at Logan Airport and managed to find him before he had made a reservation to fly to Paris to look for me.

Finally, when my fruitless Geneva adventure was over, and we were all fast asleep at home, the telephone jolted us awake at 3:00 A.M. London Airport was calling. Over my husband's shoulder, I heard the Englishman's voice, "We have been unsuccessful in locating your wife. So sorry, sir!"

"It's quite all right," my husband sleepily thanked him. "She is asleep next to me."

BACK IN WELLESLEY

AFTER I HAD been back in Wellesley for a week, Martha discovered one evening that I was getting bald.

"What do you mean I'm getting bald?" I asked, knowing well that I was losing my hair by the handful.

"You have a round spot on the back of your head with almost no hair on it," she persisted with her usual frankness. My husband, reading the paper, quipped that up till then he'd been the only bald one around the house, and now there would be two.

"It's not funny," Martha was indignant. "She's really getting bald." She asked her father to see for himself.

"Women don't get bald, silly," he said. "I have yet to see a bald woman or one who is as bold as you!"

But I was getting bald. When I held up a mirror to look at the back of my head, I saw that my hair was not just receding on top, but as Martha had said, there was a round area which showed nothing but shiny pink skin. How incredible to lose my hair! I had always had such a thick mop of natural curls. In the ensuing weeks my thinning hair was very distrubing to me.

I was home only for a couple of days when my condition worsened. I was overcome by an alarming dizziness; I didn't trust myself to walk from one room to another, and to make matters worse, the twitching of my limbs recurred. It didn't help to stand, sit, or lie flat. In bed I had to roll from side to side, trying to find a position in which I could relax. The spot on my arm where I had been vaccinated a few weeks before pained me like an angry boil. When I called up Dr. Gardner, he was mostly puzzled by the description of my sore. I mentioned to him the passing comment of the young doctor in Geneva, namely, that I should not have been vaccinated.

"He might be right," Dr. Gardner said. "I've thought of it myself. It's hard to know where to draw the line with you. In your case anything can trigger a hypersensitive reaction."

He made an appointment for me to see him the next day. Before he hung up the receiver, he repeated his intention to start me on the nicotinic acid by injection very soon. He had not heard from the Bulgarian doctors.

At my next appointment, the LE prep Dr. Gardner took was positive for the first time. Dr. Diamond also examined the cell. However, in the latter's opinion, the test result was still not definitive. This difference in opinion was enough to sustain my hope.

Dr. Gardner decided to withdraw the cortisone slowly and he stopped the white-cell injections. I was to continue with 250 mg. of hydroxychloroquine, and he began to give me 1 cc of nicotinic acid intravenously daily for the next month. This was known as the Bulgarian medicine in the lab. Dr. Gardner told me of another patient of his who, with a serious blood disease, was doing extremely well on herbs. The woman insisted on drinking tea made out of violets.

I answered that Bulgarians were known for being fond of herbs. We had a story about an herb doctor who practiced folk medicine in a village. A peasant came to him complaining of a stomachache, and the herb doctor brewed some herbs for him. When the peasant returned to report that he was all well, the herb doctor wrote in his notebook that the herb cures stomachaches. A few days later, a priest came to see him, likewise complaining of a stomachache, and the herb doctor brewed the same herbs for him. The priest died shortly after, and the herb doctor added in his notebook that the potion is no good for priests.

After two weeks of the new regimen of hydroxychloroquine and nicotinic acid, I showed a marked improvement; the glands on my neck regressed substantially, and the redness of my face faded. The nausea persisted, but I imagined myself feeling somewhat stronger. The laboratory picture remained unchanged. Off and on, Dr. Gardner would ask casually if I had heard from the Bulgarian professor. I felt sure that Professor Popoff's answer had been delayed by Red red tape.

On one of my visits I showed Dr. Gardner a photostat of an article from a 1952 dermatology journal[42] which stated that priority for the use of mepacrine* in rheumatoid disease belonged to Professor L. Popoff (1941), Sofia. Dr. Gardner read the article carefully, but his response to it was noncommittal. I complained to him of the daily trips to the hospital. It was exhausting. I had to travel for twenty-five miles from Wellesley to Peter Bent Brigham and back, just for the nicotinic-acid injection. "I wish I could give my own injections," I muttered.

Dr. Gardner, who was just preparing the injection, looked at me challengingly. "Here"—he handed me the syringe—"do it yourself." He meant it. I took the syringe with uncertain hands, feeling as if I were going to commit hara-kiri, and followed his instructions. Since then, I have injected the nicotinic acid myself . . . intramuscularly. I do not have the courage to give it in the vein.

At a later date, after seeing Dr. Gardner, my

---

*Mepacrine: Quinacrine, atabrine, the antimalarial drug which was taken by United States Armed Forces personnel during World War II.

thoughts drifted to Flannery O'Connor,[43] a writer I greatly admired. In the introduction to her book, *Everything That Rises Must Converge,* Robert Fitzgerald wrote of her desperate illness. He emphasized that Flannery O'Connor did not have ordinary arthritis, but a more serious illness called lupus, a related disease that had also killed her father.

Ever since I had read that introduction, I had been worried that lupus might be genetically transferable. At times, I would wake up and worry about my children eventually being stricken with lupus. I made a mental note to ask Dr. Gardner about it when I saw him the next time. I should actually show him the book, I told myself.

Flannery O'Connor's condition seemed very close to mine. I could see her swollen face and hands. . . . I could feel her pains and helplessness. . . . She, too, was losing her hair; she, too, could hardly walk up and down the stairs. Her doctor described her illness as disseminated lupus, an autoimmune disease in the general group of arthritis and rheumatic fever—primarily a blood-vessel disease which could affect any organ; it could affect the bones, too. And the body was forming antibodies to its own tissue. . . . What a horrible thought.

When I showed Dr. Gardner Fitzgerald's introduction, he seemed to be interested in the medical part. I told him how worried I was about my children's getting lupus someday. He replied that he was not aware of large-scale genetic studies on this problem. If such familial incidence could be established, he thought that it would aid in understanding the cause of systemic lupus erythematosus. He commented that several cases had been reported in medical journals of siblings developing lupus, but the reports were too sporadic to be conclusive. Nevertheless, relatives of lupus patients often had symptoms or positive laboratory tests for rheumatoid arthritis, a disease which is in some way related to LE.[44]

Before I left his office, I complained again of my nausea. "Everything I eat makes me sick, but milk affects me the worst. Whenever I eat dairy products, I get diarrhea and abdominal cramps, as well as nausea."

"Milk intolerance is uncommon," he said, "but some people cannot digest an important ingredient in milk called lactose." He reflected for a moment. "You might be able to have some cheeses which contain only a trace of lactose."

"Is there a test to prove sensitivity to milk?" I asked.

"Yes," he said, "they do one all the time at Children's Medical Center. It's time consuming," he warned.

"May I have the test?"

"I don't see why not. You'll have to come to the hospital one morning before breakfast; the test takes a few hours." He reflected for a moment. "Come in at seven thirty tomorrow morning. We'll determine once and for all if you are sensitive to milk."

The next day, Arthur, by then taller than I and on holiday from school, offered to give me a ride to the hospital. In the parking lot behind the hospital, we stopped to look at the trailer, Dr. Gardner's new acquisition. He had purchased the thing to expand the office space for his research team, who were crowded three and four to a room. This new gypsy-style addition was an innovation for the Harvard Medical area. Fortunately, it was hidden within a courtyard of the hospital. Had it been perched more visibly it would have detracted from the landmark surrounding it. I was told it had to be lowered into place by a derrick.

Arthur left the hospital, promising to pick me up at noontime when the test would be over. As soon as I walked into Dr. Gardner's congested lab, he gave me a fair amount of lactose sugar to drink, then a technician took blood from my right arm. She did this about five times at measured intervals. Toward 10:30 A.M., I began to have severe diarrhea. I was so nauseated that I had to rest my head in my lap. By 12:00, when the test was finished, my knees buckled and I crumbled in a chair bathed in cold sweat. One of Dr. Gardner's young assistants rushed for a stretcher, but by the time he returned, I felt somewhat better.

"You didn't have to go that far to prove your point," Dr. Gardner teased as I sipped some tea in his office.

The results of the tests showed that after taking the lactose sugar I had no elevation of my blood glucose, the normal sugar of the blood. I tolerated a mixture of glucose and galactose* without any stress. Dr. Gardner admitted that I must have had a lifelong intolerance of lactose. Lactose could not be taken up directly by the intestine, he said. It had to be first broken down by an enzyme† called lactase into two simple sugars—glucose and galactose. These smaller molecules could be absorbed more easily.

In the past, Dr. Gardner had prescribed innumerable drugs to control my nausea, but nothing had worked. I had already taken Sparine, Bendectin, codeine, Dimetapp, Serpasil, and atropine. "Try caffeine-free coffee," he said. "Forget your Turkish coffee for a while." He knew that I made coffee the way my father did in the old country and that I drank it constantly. "How do you cook that stuff, anyway?" he asked.

I told him my father's recipe: a cup of water, a teaspoon of coffee, a teaspoon of sugar, and a teaspoon of love. Boil it three times over, and with some luck, it

---

*Galactose: One of the sugars in milk, a part of the lactose molecule.
†Enzyme: A protein substance that catalyzes the reaction between two other chemicals.

would come out just right, with lots of foam on top, and sediment on the bottom.

Dr. Gardner was amused and said that he would have to try it.

One day, toward the end of the summer of 1959, three months after I met Jordan, I received a reply from his sister, the physician, in Bulgaria. She confirmed her brother's diagnosis and his successful treatment with nicotinic acid. She also mentioned that Professor Popoff had written to us as well, and she advised us to write to Merck Company in Darmstadt, Germany (not associated with Merck Company in America), for their prospectus[45] (no longer available) on the treatment of lupus with nicotinic acid. Her letter did not change Dr. Gardner's opinion of the drug; he was as skeptical as ever.

I wrote to the Merck Company. They replied promptly. In a way, I was encouraged—this was the first time I saw the word "lupus" in print. I began to translate the almost forgotten German I had learned in school as a child; the words came back with magical speed. One of the articles stated that the tests which were conducted have shown, in a great number of cases, that a certain percentage of patients had good results by being treated with nicotinic acid. Sometimes the treatment brought complete remission. This was particularly true of cases which were precipitated by sunlight, even moderate exposure. It also attempted to draw a comparison between light-sensitive LE and the nicotinamide vitamin-deficiency disease called pellagra.

A morbid thought occurred to me. Should I expose myself once again to the sun to prove my light sensitivity? The following weekend when my husband and I drove to Maine to visit some friends, I held my bare arm out the window for over two hours to the mercy of the sun and the wind. The following day, big

red angry welts erupted on my skin. The spots didn't
fade for months. The experiment cost me permanent
minor scarring of my arm. The redness always becomes
intensified when I am too cold or too hot.

After one of my visits with Dr. Gardner, while my
arm was still angry-looking, a young student nurse
noticed my sore and asked me what had happened. I
told her it was a nasty sunburn. With big innocent eyes
she bubbled that she had seen a patient with an obscure
disease who had died in a matter of weeks after such a
nasty sunburn. "I didn't believe the doctors when they
said that the sun was the reason for the woman's
death," she giggled. "I love the sun, don't you?"

"Healing," Papa would tell me, "is not a science but the intuitive art of wooing Nature."[46]

—W. H. AUDEN
The Art of Healing

PROFESSOR DOCTOR LIUBEN POPOFF

PROFESSOR POPOFF'S LETTER arrived two weeks after the letter from Jordan's sister. In the left upper corner of his stationery was neatly printed in small black type:

Prof. Dr. Liuben Popoff
Directeur de la Clinique Dermatologique
de la Faculté
Rue Marin Drinov 9
Sofia, Bulgaria

I looked at the French title and wondered for a moment, then told myself that he was probably trained in France. Writing in Bulgarian and in longhand, he showed friendly concern and eagerness to help me. What a joy, after having waited impatiently for three months. First, Professor Popoff wrote, he needed the answers to a series of questions:

1. How are your stomach, liver, and kidneys functioning?
2. What do the blood tests show specifically with regard to the lupus erythematosus cells?
3. Do you have any local infections?

110

4. What is the condition of your heart and your endocrine system?
5. How are you affected by the seasons, solar rays, and other external factors?
6. What are the histopathological* findings so far?
7. What is the condition of your nervous system with respect to the vasomotor† functions? Are you restless, acrocyanotic?‡
8. What have the doctors done for you so far, and how have you been tolerating the treatments?

In reply to our inquiry about the nicotinic acid and its therapeutic value in lupus, he said (in rough translation), that the cause and development of the disease had occupied him and his collaborators for over thirty years. He saw an analogy between pellagra and some forms of lupus, which he described as pellagroid types. For more information, he referred us to some of his papers,[47] which had appeared in various medical journals.

He wrote further that in 1944, he introduced the treatment of LE with antimalarials.[48] Finally, he said that for many years in his clinic they had used the combined treatment of antimalarial drugs and the nicotinic acid. This treatment gave good results in most forms of lupus but excellent results in the cases which are made worse by sunlight (the pellagroid type). In acute stages of the disease which he called lupovisceritis, he recommended adrenal hormones, gamma globulins, perfusions of plasma, vitamin B_{12}, and nicotinic acid. He also referred to his paper read at the Congress of

---

*Histopathology: Change in tissues and cells.
†Vasomotor: Pertaining to control of the tone of the blood vessels. Contraction of blood vessels causes blanching, whereas relaxation causes blushing.
‡Acrocyanosis: Mottled blue discoloration of the skin of the extremities.

Leningrad in 1960. He felt encouraged with the good results that Dr. Gardner and I had obtained so far with the new regimen of nicotinic acid and hydroxychloroquine. He was pleased by our interest in his research. "Keep me posted," he urged, "on how you progress with the nicotinic-acid treatments. I expect you to feel even better as time goes on." His words were tremendously reassuring to me.

As I read the letter to him, Dr. Gardner listened patiently but could not hide his skepticism. However, in the months that followed, his skepticism was replaced with curiosity as my illness changed its course. He even expressed a desire to read some of the lupus case histories that Professor Popoff must have accumulated over the years.

Each day I felt myself getting better, but the nausea persisted. Two weeks after I got Professor Popoff's letter, I wrote to him again and mentioned my nausea. He replied immediately, explaining that some lupus patients have digestive problems. He advised taking ten drops of hydrochloric acid and a teaspoon of Pepsencia* with breakfast each morning. He wrote that I probably lacked some digestive juices in my stomach and added that this was not uncommon with patients who had problems similar to mine. I translated this to Dr. Gardner and he explained that after the food and water enter the stomach, they mix with gastric juices to start the digestive processes. The essential constituents of these juices are an acid (hydrochloric) and two or possibly three enzymes (digestive ferments) called pepsin, rennin, and lipase. The medicines containing those substances were old-fashioned patent remedies and could be bought without a prescription. He agreed with

---

*Trade name for a medicine containing stomach digestive enzymes.

Professor Popoff that at some point I should have my digestive juices tested.

A few days after I took the Pepsencia, the nausea stopped. What bliss! In the morning, I used to lie in bed with my eyes closed enjoying the sensation of being well. I was afraid to open them for fear I was dreaming. It took time for my family to get used to my coming into the kitchen before anyone else was up to prepare breakfast.

After I had about sixty nicotinic-acid injections, the clinical picture turned around. To the surprise of even the kidney specialist at Peter Bent Brigham, my kidneys were getting better, too.

Because Dr. Gardner constantly spoke with me in medical terminology, I developed a fair comprehension of what was going on. Thus, when he said, "Your BUN is eight milligrams percent and the creatimine clearance is improving sharply," I knew that things were better. For only a few months previously, the BUN had been 50 mg. percent, a level seen just before the last stages of Bright's disease,[49] kidney failure. Further, he added confidently, "The LE prep is negative and even the white-cell count is going up and has reached five thousand."

The sores healed. The red butterfly went away. The hair on my scalp grew back thicker than ever. I never had to wear the wig I had secretly bought from a department store in Boston. The color of my newly grown hair was slightly changed; it was a shade lighter and grayish at the temples. I had read somewhere that this could happen to people with blond hair, after they have been on prolonged therapy with hydroxychloroquine. I certainly was glad it was my hair and not my eyes that were affected. Every time I had swallowed the medicine I had fears of becoming blind. I had had such bad luck with drugs.

One evening, when I played tennis for half an hour under the electric lights of the Wellesley public courts, my whole family came to watch. When, at the end of the set, I didn't drop dead, I knew that from then on, my life would change for the better. The next day, my husband rushed to buy me a new tennis racket.

The next four years brought good health. My ordeal seemed to be over. Once more I became interested in activities outside the house. I went back to Peter Bent Brigham to do volunteer work a few hours a week and I joined the League of Women Voters in Wellesley. The newly formed Committee on the Development of Human Resources captured my imagination. My enthusiasm led me to become a member of the board and I put all my heart into running the committee. However, the prolonged illness with all its uncertainties had left me somewhat unsure of myself. I lacked confidence when I made an appointment; I was always afraid I wouldn't be able to keep it. It took some months, even years, before I outgrew those fears completely.

The clinical picture remained stable. The only drugs I was taking were the nicotinic-acid injections and the many vitamin pills. Dr. Gardner still came across a "rare and atypical" LE cell, "an undernourished one," as he enjoyed saying, as if to denigrate its importance.

I kept in close correspondence with Professor Popoff who continued to be extremely friendly and cooperative. It was late April when he wrote that he had been invited to an international dermatological congress in Lyon, France, in two weeks, and I became terribly tempted to go and meet him. I saw an opportunity to thank the man in person and also possibly to learn a little more about lupus. My husband began a tactical campaign to encourage the new venture. Dr. Gardner was also in favor of my taking the trip. He was still interested in getting some of Professor Popoff's case histories, teasing me about my "Bulgarian treatment," while persistently attributing my getting well to a spontaneous remission.*

The first week in May, I wrote to Professor Popoff that I was considering taking the trip to Lyon. I reasoned with myself that I should take this trip—I had to find out more about lupus. I vacillated until it was actually time for me to leave.

That same week my husband and I had supper with a couple, old friends in Cambridge, and I mentioned that I was toying with the idea of meeting Professor Popoff in Lyon. Zelda, who had never been to Europe, said wistfully that, if she were in my place, she wouldn't have to think twice about it. Her husband suggested that Zelda and I should travel to Lyon together. We all agreed in a sudden burst of enthusiasm.

On May 15, 1960, at 8:00 P.M., Zelda and I boarded a Pan American plane at Logan Airport in Boston. The next morning we landed in Paris and stayed at the Louvois for two days. I did more walking in these forty-eight hours than I had done in many years. I couldn't believe my own energy.

On the train to Lyon, most of the passengers were amputees. Every seat was occupied by a man lacking one limb or another. We watched them with an odd nervousness. The station in Lyon was a nightmare; in the bright sunlight thousands of cripples seemed to haunt the platform. On the way to the hotel, our bewilderment grew into horror. The streets were crowded with men in wheelchairs, on crutches, lacking an arm or arms, or dragging artificial legs.

"I am losing my wits," Zelda nudged me in the taxi. A little later, she whispered, "Whatever is happening

---

*A spontaneous remission describes a change in the course and severity of a disease which occurs without medical intervention.

here, it seems to strike only men." For the rest of the ride we didn't say a word. We should have had the sense to inquire what was going on, but we didn't. In our hotel room we saw a large, wrapped box on the table. It was addressed: "Amputee Marcel Le Rouge."

"I'll bet it's an artificial arm or leg," Zelda eyed the box suspiciously.

I didn't like the size of it, either. Just then there was a knock. When I opened the door, a man with only one arm clumsily asked if there was a package for him left by mistake in our room. He explained that there was much confusion in town with thousands of amputees, veterans of World War II, attending a congress. I placed the parcel under his arm, then watched him go down the corridor to the elevator. I was drawn to his tragedy in the same way as with the man at Chamonix. Was he still alive? Somehow I felt the three of us shared a common bond, that of unnecessary man-made diseases. The lung damage from dust in the tunnel, the arm lost in battle, the disease made worse by drugs—all of these were avoidable problems in a life which had an abundance of the unavoidable to deal with.

When I slowly closed the door, Zelda was frantically calling from the bathroom. Examining the facilities, she could not figure out how to operate the toilet. I explained to her that she was looking at the French bidet. The newly remodeled and strikingly redecorated modern bathroom, tiled in black and white, had everything except a toilet. We searched everywhere—I even poked the walls for a concealed door. Eventually, we did locate what we were searching for, outside our room near the elevator. It accommodated all the guests on our floor, ladies and gentlemen alike. Zelda and I agreed to stand watch by the door while the other was using the facilities.

Almost immediately after my arrival in Lyon, I got

on the phone to locate Professor Popoff; I only knew the name of the congress. When, after a half hour of fruitless inquiry, I found no one who could identify such a congress, I became worried. I had already called the medical school, the chamber of commerce, and several newspapers. Nobody seemed to know what I was talking about. When I phoned the medical school for the third time, it was almost 5:00 P.M. This time, the switchboard operator had a vague idea about the meeting, which she thought was taking place somewhere outside Lyon. She advised me to call the following morning for more information. I knew from Professor Popoff's letters that he would be in Lyon for only three days: I had spent one in Paris, and now the second day was gone. This was incredible. I had the uneasy feeling that for the second time in two years I would have an unrewarding trip to Europe.

In the morning, struggling with another telephone operator at the medical school, my French faltered altogether. It always did when I was frustrated. Out of patience, I repeated my question loudly in English, and the response was instantaneous. The girl gave me all the information I needed in perfect English.

At 11:00 A.M., I went to meet Professor Popoff at his hotel. In the lobby, to my surprise, I found not only Professor Popoff, but Mrs. Popova as well. They were both equally delightful and equally surprised to see me looking so well—they couldn't quite believe that I was the patient from America. I looked much too healthy and energetic to fit the image they had created.

Mrs. Popova was a large woman with a pleasant face and an almost shy smile. She wore a simple cotton dress and flat shoes. Her French was poor, but she managed to make herself understood.

Professor Popoff, wearing a dark suit and a French beret tilted over his silvery hair, looked more like a

Frenchman than a Bulgarian. He, too, was on the heavy side.

"My dear lady," he exclaimed in perfect French, "you look marvelous! Frankly, I expected to see . . ."

I gave him my hand and told him that I hadn't always looked as healthy as I did now.

Mrs. Popova was the first to remember that we could all be speaking Bulgarian, our native tongue. I found it hard to address him as Mr. Professor Dr. Popoff, in the Bulgarian and European tradition, but he seemed to enjoy his titles, even though he lacked the stiffness and aplomb of the Geneva doctors. It crossed my mind that he would not be called all that in Bulgaria, now that the Communists had taken over. He suggested we have lunch together and delay the medical consultation until that evening after the meetings. Lyon was his city—he had graduated from medical school there. Nostalgically, he enumerated a few of Lyon's choice restaurants including the "four star" ones.

Over lunch, we spoke of trivial matters. I guessed his age to be close to sixty, and he had mischievously gay eyes. Between courses, he told amusing stories of his student days in Lyon. We laughed. It was such fun.

"You laugh easily," Professor Popoff remarked. "What kept you going during your illness?"

"I don't know. My spirit never broke down. Maybe it's genetic. My mother had a will of iron."

"That may have helped more than you think. I like to see patients put up a strong fight. It helps the medical treatments to work. I am sure of it. It also helps me. The physician's spirit is reinforced by a brave patient. Nature, when she turns against you, is a strong enemy. The doctor searches for allies. He first looks to the patient. Your Professor Gardner, he must have found strength in your spirit and you must have trusted him and drawn strength from his optimism. Is that not so?"

"Yes, yes," I reflected out loud. Dr. Gardner and I had been allies, neither of us knowing just what to expect from day to day. This uncertainty had in a strange way helped me. The atypical LE cells, the friendly disagreements among my physicians, the confusion in the literature, all held out the hope that I would fool everyone and get better.

It was a beautiful sunny day. Walking back to the hotel we crossed a bridge over the Rhône. I could see in the distance the Saône River, too. The view was perfectly lovely. The city had an ancient look with innumerable shimmering gold cathedral domes and ornamented bridges. I remembered some of my French history, and looking over the point of confluence where in the ripples the bright sunlight was reflected, I could almost feel Emperor Agrippa's spirit haunting the banks of the Rhône and the restless soul of Augustus following in his shadow. Professor Popoff remarked that the capital of the Celtic Gauls had changed very little since Napoleon had rebuilt it in the nineteenth century.

Professor Popoff saw me shielding the sunlight from my face and said that I should be wearing a widebrimmed hat. "No need to ask for trouble," he cautioned.

I explained that I was covered with a protective film of sun cream, and fumbled in my purse to show him the Doak Solar Cream I always carried.

He looked at the label and read, "Para-aminobenzoic acid, titanium dioxide, magnesium stearate. It looks all right. It must have some healing effect as well," he said and handed it back. As we walked along, he asked me if I had always been sensitive to the sun.

I responded by showing him the scarring on my arm and told him that I had done it on purpose to experiment and prove my photosensitivity to the sun.

"That was a dangerous thing to do," he said. "You shouldn't flirt with the sun."

I asked him if my photosensitivity was an aggravating feature or a basic factor in my disorder.

He looked at my arm from the corner of his eyes and said that in my case it might be both. He added, affirming the views of Dr. Gardner and Professor de Malraux's assistant, that a condition like mine could be acquired by a response to light of certain wave lengths.[50] In his opinion, artificial ultraviolet rays were just as harmful. These rays, too, could produce systemic reactions and progression of the disease. Abnormal photosensitivity was one of medicine's most neglected areas, he said, and more research was needed to establish a connection with human diseases, particularly lupus erythematosus. He also said that some clinicians seem to think that an abnormal reaction to light is only an aggravating and not a basic feature in LE. He shrugged and then added, "It will be very difficult scientifically to prove a relationship."

I commented that in my case, sunlight and cold[51] not only affected my skin, but also mirrored how sick I felt after the exposure. My skin needed protection from heat, cold, wind, sunlight—anything that touched it. I related an episode when I had plunged into a swimming pool that wasn't heated. "I was almost in shock," I said. "My body turned navy blue and I couldn't breathe normally for a while." In the winter I would never dream of going to bed without a hot-water bottle.

Professor Popoff explained that in some instances cold could cause an allergic reaction the same way lobster or strawberries affect some people.[52] A cold sensitivity,[53] or cryopathy, as it is called in medical language, could conceivably precipitate lupus, he said. The rash that I got from the sun, or the blue blotches from the cold, indicated parallel changes in my system. The skin's reaction was more spectacular, while the reaction of the internal organs was more dangerous. "You must be a terribly allergic person," he concluded.

After some moments he added, "Climate has an effect on health. It takes only a small temperature change to alter the course of a respiratory infection. You know that. When you have a cold, you instinctively try to keep warm," he said. "Rest is important, too. You must take care and rest as much as possible." He had a winning way about him. So far, Mrs. Popova had not interrupted him once. He went on, "Rest is an old-fashioned remedy for healing lupus and other diseases, but being of the old school, I still believe in it. For that matter, emotional balance is just as important, and so is good nourishment."

He paused for a moment. "In sensitivities like yours, certain foods can cause trouble and others should not be omitted. You probably know the foods that do not agree with you better than Professor Gardner or I do. But you must always keep in mind that a balanced diet is important in fighting all diseases. Do you eat enough fresh vegetables or are you addicted to canned foods and those foolish crash diets? I hope that being a few pounds overweight does not trouble you. As long as you do not carry it to extremes, being a little plump is better than eating an abnormal diet."

I responded defensively in an American way that in Wellesley we lived close to a farm where we could buy all the fresh vegetables we wanted. "They also sell fresh eggs and flowers that smell like flowers," I said.

The Popovy chuckled.

That evening I visited Professor Popoff as a patient. Mrs. Popova had gone out with some friends. The badly lighted hotel room was furnished with awkward old pieces of furniture. I noticed a pink and red flowered porcelain basin and pitcher standing on a tall table in the corner. The hotel was so old that I wondered if it had running water. Externally, it had a pavilion style which had a vague structural similarity to the Peter Bent Brigham Hospital. I half expected to see a trailer on the side street, housing the offices of the hotel officials.

"Make yourself comfortable," Professor Popoff pointed to a sagging chair near a low table out of which he had improvised a working desk. His light tone of earlier in the day had changed to a medical approach. The few letters he had received from Dr. Gardner and me over the past few years were spread out in front of him. The room was hot and stuffy despite the two open windows. His face, streaked with perspiration, looked tired in the dim light, but his eyes were alert. "How do you feel?" He asked the familiar question, but he corrected himself almost immediately. "You look delightfully well. It's a pleasure to see someone with such an abundance of zeal."

"Thank God, I have been feeling well for some time now," I said. "I have forgotten, or almost forgotten, how it used to be when I couldn't lift my feet from the ground. I shudder when I remember the bizarre feeling I had in my legs—they used to feel heavy, very heavy. Now I wake up in the morning looking forward to the day!"

He looked down at the pile of letters and at notes he had written to refresh his memory, then said, sounding like all the doctors in Boston, "You were placed on salicylate therapy, vitamin therapy, hormones, strepto-coccus vaccine, penicillin and white-cell injections. I've never heard of the white-cell treatment before." He speculated that injecting blood might be a stressful situation, raising the patient's own steroid level.[54] After we'd covered some familiar ground, he questioned me with meticulous care. Halfway through the conversa-tion, he remarked that whatever ailed me must have started much earlier than I or anyone else suspected. He reasoned that my problems flared up when my resistance was low. "You must have strong genes, my dear lady," he nodded. "That must be the secret of your recovery."

Later in the evening, Mrs. Popova came in, nodded a friendly greeting, and settled in an armchair by the window with a sigh of fatigue. Professor Popoff continued talking, undisturbed by her presence. "After ten years of multiple symptoms and minor clinical findings, you appear entirely well again and you don't seem to have any visible scars to account for your experience. From the letters I've received from your Professor Gardner, I understand that at one point you had kidney involvement which has cleared completely. One has to accept your case for what it is at the moment, simply that you feel well. The rest is really of academic interest." He wiped away the perspiration that had accumulated in the creases below his eyes and said, "Recovery from lupus does not mean the disease will not return. You will always have the predisposition for it." Parenthetically, he recommended a periodic chest X ray, which set me to thinking about tuberculosis. I recalled reading in a medical dictionary that lupus, at least in one of its forms, was a skin disorder caused by tuberculosis bacteria. This interested me at the time, because several uncles of mine had died of tuberculosis. I asked Professor Popoff to clear up my confusion.

He replied that tuberculosis was mistakenly believed to be a causative factor in systemic lupus erythematosus. However, he added that, more important, there was a type of lupus called lupus vulgaris,[55] a form of tuberculosis of the skin. Tuberculosis infection often ran a serious course in patients with lupus, particularly those on cortisone.

I knew such a case—a young woman from Australia

who came to Boston to consult the hematology doctors at Peter Bent Brigham, only to learn that Dr. Gardner had gone to Europe. Ironically, I had had a similar experience when I had gone to Geneva, and now I was in Lyon, still trying to find out something more about the disease.

The Australian was from a part of New South Wales where the sun shone, unmercifully for a lupus patient, 360 days a year. Her family ran a sheep station, a ranch of five thousand acres.

One of Dr. Gardner's assistants worked up her case and concluded that the disease was running a rapid course. Having compassion for the soft-spoken, trusting girl, he wondered whether a touch of the unusual—a visit with me, a "cured" lupus case—would give her hope. When he referred her to me, he suggested that we had wool interests as well as lupus in common, and whimsically asked whether I would put her on nicotinic acid. I responded to his phone call as members of Alcoholics Anonymous must respond to one another— by rushing in to Dr. Gardner's office to meet her and taking her to my house. She looked frail and could barely walk unattended.

In our living room, over a cup of tea, she told me that she'd been on large doses of prednisone for several years. She also indicated a squeamishness about giving herself nicotinic-acid shots, which would have been necessary because of the remoteness of her ranch from medical care. She was grateful to talk with me, though, and left for home with some hope.

After the young woman left our house, one of my teen-age daughters commented that she had never realized that at one time I could have been as sick as this poor woman. My other daughter thought that the patient and I looked somewhat alike. She, too, admitted that she had not been aware of the seriousness of my illness, except when I had to go to the hospital. She used to get frightened and reasoned with herself that there was nothing that she could do, but she had never been completely sure of that. She managed to laugh now. But I knew how difficult it must have been on all of them.

Upon the return of the Australian to Melbourne, we kept in touch. Her sickness grew progressively worse. My last letter was answered by her mother. I recalled her words, "Leslie received your letter before she passed away. She died of pulmonary tuberculosis."

Rising, Professor Popoff put his glasses on to examine my face. There was nothing abnormal to see. My skin was perfectly clear.

"The rash I used to have on my face was diagnosed as a typical LE rash," I said, and asked him if all lupus rashes were alike.

He said that the skin involvement in both the chronic discoid form and the acute type of SLE were just about the same: both were easily confused with other types of skin conditions.

I made a point to tell him that the doctors in Boston were skeptical of the usefulness of the nicotinic acid. "They don't understand why in the world it should work."

"Does anyone know why an aspirin relieves pain or why the cortisone performs so well?"

In the course of our conversation, I reminded him that I had been feeling well now for over five years. "It's a miracle," I said.

"It's not a miracle," he countered. He reiterated very slowly as if to give emphasis that in his experience with the lupus disease, he had found that certain patients who reacted strongly to sunlight acted similarly to those who had pellagra. He accepted that such patients were suffering from pellagroid lupus and most of them responded favorably to nicotinic acid, the way I did. He reflected for a moment. "On the other hand, your doctors in Boston have all the right in the world to be skeptical about attributing your remission to this simple medicine. One of the characteristic features of lupus is a high incidence of spontaneous remissions. Some of these remissions last indefinitely. I have records of patients who have been in remission for thirty years without any kind of therapy.

"How wonderful," I exclaimed. "Except for Jordan, I have not heard of long remissions. Just hearing about them is exciting."

He continued by saying that in my case it would be almost impossible to decide if my emission was spontaneous or induced. I had been on steroids, autogenous vaccines, antimalarials, penicillin, many vitamins, including nicotinic acid, and the white-cell injections. He also stressed that in my case, I was lucky to have had help in the house and could afford medical care. "Rest is vital," he repeated. Then he paused and added, "Even though I am a nicotinic-acid enthusiast, I must admit that lupus is an unpredictable adversary."

I mentioned that a doctor at Peter Bent Brigham had told me once to get rid of my ovaries if I wanted to get well. He was not a lupus specialist, but he was impressed with the sex distribution of the disease and wondered if decreased hormone production would help. Dr. Gardner, too, at some point of my illness, had also wondered if female hormones could influence the lupus. But he never got around to advising an operation or hormone therapy.

"The influence of female hormones has intrigued many investigators because so few men get the disease. And one obvious element of the difference is the sex hormones. But our understanding stops right there. It would be nice if someone could show how the female hormone is the troublemaker in lupus. There are ways of controlling the hormones. Anyway, I hope that lupus gets more attention in research. It seems to be a more common problem than when I started in medicine. That could be the result of better diagnosis, but somehow I feel that there are other factors bringing out the disease. Maybe it is the increased use of drugs." He shook his head a little. "The pharmaceutical industry has been very successful in making new drugs in the past thirty years. And when drugs are around, doctors and patients will use them. Every drug will find a patient who reacts badly to it. Even so, any time I see a drug reaction, I think of lupus." He paused. "You didn't react too well to cortisone, did you?"

"No, I didn't. My rash and swollen glands didn't subside until I took the nicotinic acid."

He went on in a professional manner, not looking at me directly, while pacing the floor with the exaggerated stride of the seasoned lecturer, his hands clasped and his fingers nervously twitching behind his back.

"Systemic lupus erythematosus and rheumatoid arthritis have so much in common. Even great clinicians with years of experience are fooled by one of the diseases masquerading as the other. It used to be said years ago that syphilis was the great imitator. It could mimic almost all other diseases. Now, if syphilis is treated early enough with penicillin, there are fewer late complications. Today the great imitators are connective-tissue diseases—rheumatoid arthritis, lupus, and other diseases like them. They can do anything. Believe me, they can affect any part of the body. They can even make you crazy without giving obvious trouble on the skin, in the kidneys, or anywhere else. Connective-tissue disease is a very clever opponent for the clinician. That is why your Boston professors took so long to prove your diagnosis. This is not to criticize them. This is really to praise them for their stamina."

I reminded him that these uncertainties about my sickness had originally given me strength to fight for survival. "I clung to the doctors' lack of knowledge about lupus as a drowning man clings to a straw," I had to laugh.

He said that the fact that I was responding so well to the nicotinic acid led him to believe that I might have a deficiency of nicotinic acid. "I have the feeling that your system does not use nicotinic acid efficiently. This would cause you to need more of it to do the same job that it does for most people. I came to this belief because of my experience with pellagra, which you may not know is common in some parts of the Balkans. Why, I don't know. There is so much good food there. The light sensitivity of pellagra goes away immediately with nicotinic-acid treatment.

"My reasoning was simple. If it helps one light-sensitive disease, it could help another. Simple thought, wasn't it? But the results have sometimes been remarkable. As in your case, I have seen many people helped by this simple vitamin." He handed me a slip of paper with a few more questions for Dr. Gardner to answer and told me that in my case the treatment should be limited to the use of skin preparations of cortisone, sun-screening creams, and the nicotinic-acid injections. He urged me to stay on those injections indefinitely, but on an intermittent basis. "Let's say"—his tone reminded me now of Dr. Gardner's—"you should take the injections for a month or two, then rest for a few weeks before starting up again. Eat good plain food, and stay away from spicy, salty dishes. Salt is apt to retain fluids in your tissues." He paused briefly. Then he said, "Even if you have a relapse some day, I feel that you will overcome it. I believe that many people have a quiet form of lupus, and we bring out their disease by giving them too many medicines for innocent complaints. Then the medicine leads to new complaints and we chase the problem with new medicine. We begin to believe that the patient is neurotic. The neurosis starts or finishes our chase. It is difficult to tell for sure in some patients."

He made me wonder if many women who were called neurotic really had a touch of lupus with no red butterfly to prove it. I knew only too well how one could be affected by the bizarre turns of the illness. I remembered the days when I would see double, or wake up at night with the strange sensation that both my arms were gone. I remembered how, reaching for the telephone receiver, I wasn't sure that I could speak, and the floating sensation I used to experience in West Newton when the radiators appeared distorted and I had dreaded focusing on them ... and the skin spots I used to get: red ones, pink ones, blue ones; the little bumps that came and vanished before I had had a chance to reach the doctor's office. Thank God, those days were over!

Professor Popoff glanced at his watch. It was midnight. "You must be feeling tired," he said. "I know I am." Mrs. Popova, who suddenly woke up, was surprised to see me standing next to her husband. She looked weary and disheveled.

"I should have gone long ago," I held out my hand to her. She took it warmly in both of hers, and in a gesture of kindness, invited me to visit them in Bulgaria the next time I came to Europe. Her husband repeated her words and said to forget about lupus ... as much as possible.

"You can see that she has done that," Mrs. Popova said and squeezed my hands once more.

Professor Popoff promised me that as soon as he

received more information from Professor Gardner, he would go over my case once again and further search for clues to explain my remission. As he spoke, I mentioned that Dr. Gardner had asked to see some of Professor Popoff's lupus case histories. He made a note of my request. I thanked the Popovy heartily and we embraced in the French manner, which was most unusual for Bulgarians who are not by nature a demonstrative people.

After I left the Popovy, I walked slowly back to my hotel. The boulevard by the Rhône was brightly lighted by the moon. The town seemed deserted and the soft splashing of water made sounds of peaceful dreaming. The rhythm of my steps kept the strange magic alive. The tired feeling I would have had in the past was now a memory. I felt nothing more than a healthy weariness.

Professor Popoff's words returned to my mind. Everything he told me sounded reassuring. I realized that the violence of my earlier emotional reaction to the disease had disappeared and so I was no longer preoccupied with the thought of early death. Since my arrival in Lyon, the future looked brighter than ever. Back at the hotel, I tiptoed into my room where Zelda was asleep with the lights on. Thinking it was morning, she opened her eyes and asked me eagerly what Professor Popoff had said.

As I undressed, I told her that everything about the disease was nebulous. Professor Popoff had even suggested that I had something like pellagra. Me, pellagra? I liked the sound of pellagra. The long "a" gave it a certain rhythm. He called it pellagroid lupus—lupus looking like pellagra. "I guess I'll live," I said. Then I added, "When I go back to the States, I'll tell my doctors to do more research on light waves of harmful strength in connection with photosensitivity." Then I mumbled, "Why do all doctors talk to me as though I could understand their 'lingua medicina'?"

"They always do that when they're at sea about an illness," Zelda replied with the authority of a doctor's wife. "They must hate the sound of lupus as much as you do."

I put out the lights and asked her how she had spent the day.

"You're taking your sickness with a lot more equanimity than I would have thought possible," she said between yawns. "I don't know what I would have done if I had to cope with lupus."

"Be glad that you don't have to," I said. For a while I tried to listen to her sudden bubbling enthusiasm as she described a pink lettuce in a garden that she mistook for a giant rose, but I soon fell asleep.

The next morning we packed hurriedly and drove for two hours to Voiron to see the Landrus. After spending two delightful days with them, Zelda and I continued to Switzerland. Now, Geneva appeared enchanting in contrast to the ghastly week I had spent there several years before.

At Orly Airport in Paris, Zelda and I boarded a plane crowded with a group of M.I.T. professors who had been studying the Common Market while touring Western Europe. They seemed to have collected every funny story available in Europe's capitals and the crescendos of their laughter interrupted our conversations over the entire Atlantic.

However, the happy atmosphere changed to apprehension when, nearing Logan Airport in Boston, word went around that I had not been inoculated for smallpox. Before I had left Boston, Dr. Gardner had decided not to give me the vaccine. Instead, he had written a letter to show the authorities, in which he explained that in lupus patients such vaccine could activate the disease. The passengers, feeding upon rumor, became jittery thinking that they might be quarantined at Logan. I was worried and self-conscious. Dr. Gardner had told me that he would be in Boston at the time of my return so that I could call him from the airport if I ran into any difficulties. Waiting in line to pass the immigration authorities, I could feel everyone looking in my direction.

After the inspector carefully read Dr. Gardner's letter, silently moving his lips to pronounce "lupus, lupus"—as if to say, "What the hell is that?"—he questioned me on my whereabouts during the last three weeks of the trip. He then left hurriedly, instructing his colleagues to keep everyone on the premises. The M.I.T. group clustered in the background, viewing the proceedings with academic curiosity and whispering knowingly among themselves. He soon returned with a doctor in military uniform who immediately released the other passengers, then walked toward me, grinning. When the doctor came closer, he immediately told me that I, too, would be released, but spoke so softly that no one responded. As I victoriously passed through the inspection area, a spontaneous cheer went up. France and Switzerland, he explained to willing ears, were the only two Western European countries which were absolutely free from smallpox. Reports of isolated cases had been coming in from several other countries. But nothing to be alarmed about.

"I shall let you go home, conditionally," he said as he handed me a piece of paper to sign. "This commits you to report to me if you develop any symptoms."

I signed the paper and gave him a smile. "With lupus, Doctor, one always has symptoms, and I would never know if I had smallpox, or just an off day!"

"Lupus is a peculiar disease, isn't it?" he mused. "I never saw a case of it in medical school or internship. Then my sister died of it in three months."

GIRLS DON'T WHISTLE!

IT WAS EARLY April, 1966, thirteen years after the
onset of lupus. The past seven or eight years had been
wonderful for us. The children had grown up, two were
in college, one in high school. We all loved our house on
Temple Road. The garden I had envisioned when we
bought the house was now a reality. The informal
arrangement of flowers were splashes of color, the way
gardens used to look in Bulgaria. I loved digging in the
damp soil. One day, while planting some rose bushes, I
became aware that I was whistling. I could not believe
it! After all these years, I could enjoy once more this
long-forgotten pleasure. Later, when I walked into the
house, still whistling, Martha looked at me surprised and
said, "Mothers don't whistle!"

"Your mother does!" I said. "She started way back in
Bulgaria!"

Although I was feeling great, I still had to take
precautions whenever the breath of spring tempted me
toward my garden—I had to beware of the sun. I did not
mind applying the Doak Solar Cream, but hated
spraying myself with insect repellent. Bugs loved me. In
1951 I had something similar to lupus in Gorham, New
Hampshire. It was during the month of June when the
black flies were at their worst. The bites got infected
and blistered and I ran a fever of over 101 degrees.

Luckily, I got over it quickly. In previous years, some doctors had suspected insect bites as a possible cause for the outbreak of my lupus—lupus has many ways of starting.

During the same afternoon that I had worked in the garden and discovered that I could whistle again, in the midst of arranging flowers in the dining room with my youngest daughter, a sudden pain gently squeezed the lower part of my chest. I grasped the edge of the table, afraid to move, but immediately felt a little better—the sequence happening too quickly for my daughter to react. By nine o'clock in the evening, the pain had increased so badly that I had to call a doctor in Wellesley to come to the house. In the short time he took to come, the pain had grown unbearable. Wiping the perspiration from my face with a turkish towel, the doctor speculated that I was having a gallbladder attack! He jabbed a needle in my thigh, drew some blood from my arm, and said I'd fall asleep in a few minutes. He promised to return first thing in the morning.

Unsure of just what a gallbladder was, I fell asleep as soon as the doctor left the room. But not for very long! At two thirty, I awoke in agony. I was rolling from side to side, moaning as if in labor, afraid that I would wake everyone in the house. By four o'clock, my husband called the doctor once more and the good man arrived in a few minutes wearing a light coat over his pajamas. After one quick look at me, he picked up the telephone and called an ambulance.

"You probably feel like crawling the walls," he said before he made a second telephone call to get a bed at Peter Bent Brigham. I was worried by the possibility that the Brigham was full. My great hospital had only three hundred beds.

A few hours later, the Brigham had me again and Dr. Gardner was, as usual, by my bedside. He, too, took blood and after I had a series of X rays, a diagnosis of cholecystitis was confirmed. I had a gallbladder full of stones. One of the stones had settled in the wrong place and caused an obstruction. Dr. Gardner stressed the need for an immediate operation. I knew that he was worried about my having major surgery. Anybody with a history like mine had to be shielded from stress, even from tooth extractions.

Four days after I entered the hospital, the operation was done. On rounds the next day, the surgeon was pleased with his handiwork. As he looked at the gastric suction bottle, he said that he hadn't seen any signs of lupus. The spleen, liver, kidneys "felt" normal, but no biopsies were taken. The gallbladder problem was as classical as it could be.

"A typical 4F's case," another doctor chortled at a medical student.

The student, who didn't know what he meant, had the l'esprit de moment to answer in the same low voice, "I am sure it doesn't apply to her draft status."

I had to laugh even though it caused a lot of pain in the incision. My surgeon glanced at his watch and waved good-bye to me as if to spare me the need to push any words through my dry mouth and lips.

I later learned what they meant by their 4F joke: fair, fat, female, forty. One of the nurses told me, half apologetically. I told her not to worry—I had become used to the Brigham. It was very much like a small town. Everyone spoke his mind—and nothing remained a secret.

The next day, Dr. Gardner was puzzled when my lips blossomed with blisters. He gradually eliminated many possibilities—and narrowed suspicion down to the disinfectant solution in which the thermometer was kept. After that, the nurses washed the thermometer in soap and water, and the sores healed. Then a rash appeared and soon covered all of my body. The drug list seemed harmless enough for a "post-op" patient: Compazine,[56] Demerol,[57] Seconal,[58] Meprospan[59]. No antibiotics. None of the usual troublemakers. Nevertheless, they stopped all drugs, gave me nicotinic-acid injections, and happily the rash went away. The gallbladder had not been as difficult to handle as my tendency to react badly to many drugs. As pointed out by the resident, I did illustrate the modern aphorism, "This is the day of safe surgery and dangerous drugs."

Professor Popoff sent me a get-well cable. In his opinion, the gallbladder could have been a hidden source of chronic infection. He expected me to feel even better than before the surgery.

President Johnson had his gallbladder out the day after my surgery. I delighted in following his daily health bulletins. But as the days went on, I began to worry about him, since I was able to attend my household chores long before he returned to the White House.

When it was time to leave the hospital, I found that I could not hire a nurse. A friend, who did volunteer work with parolees from a women's reformatory, suggested I call a Catholic organization in Boston which might be able to help. I called and spoke to Sister Frances. She became interested in my problem and even came to my house. She had someone for me—Mildred Adams, a black parolee who had lost her nursing license for pushing drugs to minors. In the few minutes Sister Frances spent with me, she was able to convey her faith in this woman. Mildred proved to be a godsend. She had healing hands and a gentle deep voice.

During the three weeks Mildred stayed with me, she frequently spoke of prison life. At first she was reluctant to talk about it. She would say, "I won't tell you—you'd just get depressed." But then she told me some of the worst. I used to stare at her, hardly able to believe her words.

Her first day at the reformatory had been a nightmare, she recollected. "I wished that day that I was dead," she confessed, with horror in her eyes.

"They beat you?"

"Jesus, no," Mildred said. Then she rushed on, "They made me take my clothes off and made me lay on a table. Two matrons grabbed my legs and stretched them apart. They cursed. They said they smelled rot. I kept saying 'Hail Mary, full of grace,' as fast as I could. The matron looked for dope inside me. She didn't wear a glove and her finger ripped me like it was a claw. It felt like she was inside my belly. I passed out when I saw her hand covered with my blood." Mildred stopped for breath, "When I came to, it was impossible to bring my legs together. My bladder was so swollen and hurt so much, I couldn't even urinate."

The agony of heroin withdrawal was another horror story Mildred told. Her job with me was the first one after she got out of jail, and she was grateful for the chance to work again. The bitterness would leave if she could only stay busy.

Mildred was the first girl I ever knew who had spent time in jail, but she was not the last. I became interested in other girls like her and found it very rewarding to give a helping hand. In Mildred's words—compassion and quick reform were desperately needed to change the archaic penal system of Massachusetts.

Suddenly everything is wrong with
you. Your symptoms are so varied,
they just can't be real.[60]
—Susan Golick Rosenblum,
President, Lupus Erythematosus
Foundation, Inc.

You asked me how I feel. Now that
I've lost both my kidneys, I hope
and pray that soon a cure will be
found to help me and others like
me to prevent the pain and hope-
lessness.
—From a letter written by
Joanne Mazarakis, a lupus sufferer.

PETER BENT BRIGHAM HOSPITAL, 1970

SEVENTEEN YEARS AFTER the onset of my disease, on May 28, 1970, I reentered Peter Bent Brigham Hospital for a routine checkup under the care of Dr. Chester Alper, who earlier had been a member of Dr. Gardner's group. Dr. Gardner in 1966 had taken a professorship in Philadelphia. He continued to direct my care from a distance, and once a year I went to Philadelphia for follow-up. Alper in Boston, Gardner in Philadelphia, Popoff in Bulgaria—wouldn't it have been nice if all of them could be in Boston together in the same hospital? No, that would take away my excuse for flying to see them, and I so very much loved to travel.

The main lobby of Peter Bent Brigham Hospital looked like a bus terminal—it was so crowded, I could hardly move about. In the coffee shop behind the huge

138

semicircular information desk every chair and table was taken and the gift shop was cluttered with books, candies, cards—gaily displayed as if to offset the struggle and sadness which must have spilled over from the sick beds less than a hundred yards away.

Many of the young doctors had beards and ear-length hair and wore pastel shirts; and several nurses were in pants suits—a sharp change in style in only a few years.

In the admitting office, a heavy-set man submerged by mounds of paper commented that the hospital nowadays was always bustling like this. Everyone had some sort of health insurance. Medicare, too, had brought more older people for treatment. "Yet, the facilities stay the same; the Brigham is not much bigger than it was in 1913 when it was built. It belongs to another age. Perhaps some day we will have a modern building. Then we will have the elevators to complain about. At least it's possible to climb to the top floor in this place—we have only three floors, you know."

Shortly, I found myself back on the Coolidge Wing in a room next to the one where I had been twice before. Previously, I had been too ill to enjoy the pleasant sunny room with large windows looking into a court-yard full of fresh grass. Even though I was in perfect health now, I was getting quite fatigued from the history and physical examination by the student, the intern, the resident, the traditional routine of the teaching hospital.

The next morning, the resident brought Dr. Thorn with him. The two entered my room at the apex of a phalanx of white suits and lab coats which quickly took up positions on three sides of my bed. Dr. Thorn looked much the same, except that now the group surrounding him appeared much younger. I noticed that his flaming red hair had been tamed by the added gray and his many freckles had melted into his skin. His eyes were a little deeper set, perhaps, a few more wrinkles around the edges, but they were just as keen as ever. His face expressed the same genial glow of friendliness.

"You look well," he said in his usual tone of voice—a blend of closeness and professional routine, which had become a part of him, and effectively conveyed a feeling of welcome to his medical service. "How do you feel?" he gave me a quick observing glance, knowing the answer.

"Wonderful," I said. "My lupus has declared a moratorium—I hope it's for good."

"Isn't it great to feel so well?" he sounded very much pleased. He turned to his students and said, "You wouldn't think now that for many years she was very ill and utterly exhausted by lupus; and through all of it, she was fully aware of the gravity of her condition."

"I still tremble at the sound of lupus," I saw the many inquisitive eyes of the students looking down on me, and said, "It wasn't all that bad. I tried to enjoy myself even during the worst times."

Dr. Thorn nodded and spoke to the group. "She has done quite a bit of research on lupus. She has a remarkable understanding of her illness."

"Perhaps the lady would give me some of her thoughts," an intense young man spoke up. "I am interested in the psychological responses of patients to chronic diseases. Although I hadn't thought of it before, LE would be a good topic. It's like multiple sclerosis. Remissions and exacerbations keep the patient in a constant state of expectancy. Could I return to talk with you?" he asked.

"I'll be glad to oblige," I replied. "I've done it before." He looked so terribly young. He must have just been starting school when I had helped that other student nearly seventeen years ago.

Dr. Thorn held out his hand as if to congratulate me

for the successful fight and at the same time to say good-bye again. I knew that he was going to retire in two years, and as I squeezed his hand, I sensed that it would probably be the last time that I would see him as chief. I did not like that feeling. It meant that both of us were getting older. Aging, as opposed to lupus, would have no remission, drugs or no drugs, vitamins or no vitamins.

As the group slowly filed out of my room, Dr. Thorn continued to philosophize about lupus. "Maybe the nicotinic acid really did reduce light sensitivity. It's always hard to prove what is going on in this disease. It is like a chameleon. Always changing. You would have to set up a careful study to get worthwhile data. Can you imagine how hard that would be? It would take a lot of cases like this one to prove a point."

As in previous times when I stayed at the hospital, many young doctors and medical students came in to see me. Although I was well, they all believed I had lupus. Ironically, this recalled that when I had been sick, they were skeptical of the LE cell, the peculiar rashes, the seemingly neurotic complaints. A bizarre turnabout, I thought. When you are sick, many believe you are not, and when you get better, your illness is spoken of as a fact. The word "remission" rolled off their tongues and mine enough times to give my case the authenticity that it never commanded during its darkest hours. The students, eagerly seeking a root cause for the problem, trying to reduce it to simple, workable terms, questioned me endlessly about the sulfa-drug story, having been told to read my case report in *The Journal of the American Medical Association*. I accepted the sulfa connection so completely—I had read the section in Meyler's book[61]—I could not believe that anyone could look on it as pure coincidence. Yet some did. They offered other explanations and brought me up to date on new literature. They treated me almost as if I were a doctor. I understood all of the terms, I quoted this and that as one of them might have done, and had fun doing so. I had returned from the gates of hell and that gave me a lot to talk about.

"How does it feel to be well again?" a psychiatrist stopped to ask me. He was curious about the adjustments a person had to make in a complete remission like mine.

"It feels wonderful," I retorted. "Health has given me back my sense of reality. When the lupus was active, it was hard to function in a normal way. Sometimes the symptoms—pain, nausea, numbness—would dominate my thoughts. Other times I would only be afraid of what was coming next. Lacking strength and lacking confidence I withdrew from the outside world into the safety of family life."

"What do you mean by safety?" he asked.

"I have a good family. They did not blame me for my sickness, they did not blame themselves or God. They tried to help me," I mused. "And they had complete faith in the doctors even when the doctors themselves did not know what was going on. I think my husband helped me to transfer worry and responsibility to the doctors' shoulders instead of carrying the burdens myself. That was very important. It gave all of us something to lean on. I became philosophical. . . ."

"Philosophical?" he repeated, constantly seeming to pick up the last word of my previous thought.

"Yes, philosophical. I lived for the moment instead of the future. I spent more time with the children than I would have if I hadn't been sick." I shrugged, "I don't know if this was good or bad. Bulgarian parents tend to be overprotective. . . ." After a moment's silence, I said, "The family and the house became my universe for a while. . . . Our social contacts decreased; the furniture, the flowers, books, and even food had deeper meaning. I constantly fought my illness. I never gave up. My family would not let me."

The doctor skillfully directed our talk. "You don't seem to feel the need to be ill any longer," he said. His elongated eyes, near-slits, surrounded by puffed cheeks, reminded me of a Buddha carving I had admired once in a Japanese temple in Kyoto.

"No, I don't want to feel ill anymore. I never did. Why should anyone want to be sick?"

"Some do," he said. "But tell me, how does your husband feel about your recovery?"

"My husband? He seems pleased, of course. The remission makes his life easier. He, too, has been released from chains."

"Chains? Do you think he resented your illness? Do you think that your relationship was adversely affected by the duration of your trouble?"

"Adversely, no. But, twenty years is a long time. Chronic sickness changes a house. It would have been easier if I had been well while the children were growing." I paused. "But in more than one way, life has been good to us. We have much to be grateful for."

"And the children?"

"They seem to have survived the ordeal, too. Ingrid is a third-grade teacher and likes working with handicapped children. She gives of herself. Our son is preparing to be a teacher, too, and Martha is a junior in college. The children seem to have a social conscience and want to relate to people. The trauma of having a chronically ill mother was not an albatross for them—at least I don't think it was. Perhaps it even helped in their development. It takes some suffering to bring out humanity. I believe that. But time will tell."

An immunologist also came to see me. Lean, intense, and very soft-spoken, he introduced himself as a research fellow who had done some work on lupus erythematosus and related diseases. Dr. Thorn suggested that he review my history. Perhaps here was a witch who would do for lupus what Withering's[62] informant did for heart disease when, three and a half centuries ago, she recommended foxglove* for dropsy.†

He seemed unusually poised for one still in a white uniform. His approach was philosophical. He came to swap tales about LE. He acted as if he would value my opinion in the same way as he would an LE expert on the boardwalk at the important Atlantic City meetings.

"When, in your opinion, did your disease start?" the young man asked in a friendly tone.

I had been asked that question many, many times. My answer had been rehearsed almost excessively, in French, English, and Bulgarian, at home and in the hospital, with students and professors. It brought forth the kind of response that an ancient Alsatian farmer might give to a traveler who asks about his experiences in the war. "Which war? Which experiences, monsieur? There were so many."

I began to reminisce, feeling that he would listen to the whole story and not judge me a fool if I rambled and even theorized a little.

As I began, I realized that my story had been restructured by the events, the opinions, and the articles in the medical literature which contributed to the totality of my confrontation with lupus. I no longer had the advantage of ignorance. I had to consider all possibilities just like a scientist. And the menu of possibilities had grown too large for me to handle with ease. The scientist is able to give more weight to some

---

*Foxglove: A plant whose leaves resemble fingers (digits).

†Dropsy: The swelling of the limbs and abdomen that results from heart failure.

things and less to others, on the basis of experimental facts. My emphasis depended on subjectivity and was thus more fragile, more personal.

I told him of the sore on my leg after taking a miracle drug. "Was it a sulfonamide?" I mused, not expecting him to answer.

"It probably was. How many miracle drugs were new in the thirties?"

"The sore did not heal for months. It was nature's warning to me. Years later, during one of my stays at Peter Bent Brigham, I was given a strong sedative. Hours after I had taken it, a sore appeared on my arm, looking exactly like the one I had had in Bulgaria. The same thing happened after the smallpox inoculation which was given to me before my first trip to Geneva in 1957. Still later, after taking tetracycline, I became covered with red blotches similar in shape and size and thickness to the sores I have just described. Luckily, the tetracycline was stopped immediately, and the blotches didn't ripen completely. These occurrences and a few others led me in retrospect to believe that I had the beginnings of lupus in Bulgaria."

Looking further into the past and letting my thoughts tumble, I wondered whether I had a genetic background which predisposed to the disease. Yet I knew of no one in the family who had anything resembling LE. Many of the earlier signs had been misunderstood. In my adolescence, Mother used to attribute some of my afflictions to a delicate constitution: constant strep throat, susceptibility to colds, recurring pneumonia, and the overreaction to mosquito bites were but a few of the problems. But Father contended that as the only daughter, I was spoiled by everyone in the family and may not have been so sick if I had not been so protected. He had a fundamentalist view of resistance to disease. He never thought of illness as something to spend time on.

The possibility of a genetic background for my disease stood out in my mind. I thought in simple terms: strong genes for this, weak genes for that. I fancied a series of barriers, of stages in LE. Those with the weak genes for resisting LE would put up a weak defense at each barrier and would get LE. In this primitive theory, everyone could get the disease, if the stimulus were strong enough.

Infections were the beginning—the first barrier. I got too many of them, my defense was weak, and I needed drugs to help me over the trouble. The drugs were the second barrier. Instead of helping, they caused new problems which were not interpreted correctly. The reactions should have been gratefully received as a warning signal from nature, not just for one drug but for all. Now I am even afraid of aspirin. Yet, for nearly twenty years I swallowed new pills and took injections passively, without thinking twice. I should have learned from experience, but along with my doctors, I had to be hit over the head with the allergic reactions many, many times before drawing the right conclusions.

"The next barrier in my simple theory," I said self-effacingly as if to appear more humble about my beliefs than I really was, "has to do with stress in life. Fatigue, poor diet, too much worry—these things can erode the last defenses. They cannot push you over by themselves. But once you are exhausted or lose your appetite or have too many problems to solve, the weaknesses of your makeup make themselves known, particularly if you are a woman. The young housewife— losing sleep over her children's sicknesses, trying to balance the budget, having a cigarette and coffee for breakfast—who has a predisposition to lupus, takes the wrong drug, stays out in the sun too long, and gets an infection which is hard to throw off, and the disease starts. Then the early symptoms, except for the butterfly, are so peculiar that they draw attention away from physical illness. The doctor thinks neurosis. The patient goes one step further and thinks herself eccentric, inadequate, sometimes half crazy. There is no communi-cation in this ignorance. The pills keep coming and are willingly taken. The barriers fall, the disease takes hold, and the diagnosis is easier to make. The doctor gets more sure of himself while the patient gets more frightened. The unpronounceable name of the disease, the bad outlook, the unknown cause, the side-effects of cortisone—all of it is so hard to understand. And the rash—you might as well have leprosy."

"I wonder how many women in the Middle Ages wore the Lazarus bell because of lupus," the young man interrupted. "Even today skin troubles, because they are easily seen, bring out unreasonable fears in people. They think of contagion, of curses, of filth, of evil, of unworthiness. Lupus puts you in a lazaretto, a medical and a psychological one. The doctor does not know what to do with you. You do not know what to do for yourself."

I remained quiet for a few moments, then I said, "What one needs with lupus is a doctor who will stick with you and give you courage. I was lucky—Dr. Gardner did that for me. He is always so full of energy and optimism. He is willing to try new things and to learn from his own mistakes. He stopped the white-cell injections when he thought they were not working and was quick to suspect that the Diamox might have given me problems. He never gave up, even when the kidneys became involved."

My listener never looked around the room, nor at his watch, nor refilled his pipe, and I went on, "As sick as I was, Dr. Gardner didn't want me to live in a 'glass house' as he would say, and encouraged me to talk to and offer help to other lupus patients. He knew the

value of sharing troubles. Who better to talk to than a
fellow sufferer? And there were many—once we started
to look. The fair Australian girl, a Wellesley College
teacher, a black woman—Anne-Mae—from Roxbury,
an artist from New Hampshire—all women, all desperately sick, sicker than I, crying out for understanding
as much as for medical help.

"When I first talked of the nicotinic acid, Dr. Gardner
listened, not because he believed in it—he may not
believe in it even now—but because he realized that it
was therapeutic for me to seek ways to help myself.

"He asked me to gather the literature on the subject,
cleverly referring to my 'valuable experience as a library
worker' and encouraged contacts with Professor Popoff. He revealed strength when he admitted medical
ignorance of lupus. He was conventional in using
prednisone and sun cream, but unconventional in trying
the Bulgarian remedy.[63]

"Most   importantly,   Dr.   Gardner   was   persistent . . . and he won. I should say we won; I was a good
patient."

"Yes," the young doctor said absently. Perhaps he
was thinking of the chemical reactions of nicotinic
acid[64] or the definitions of a good clinician[65] or the role
of inheritance in lupus or the preventive-medicine theme
of the drug-reaction side of the story.

None of it was new to him, but the whole package,
the interwoven tale of twenty years with LE, was
entirely new. He groped for a simple explanation, a
unifying concept, but failing that, accepted it as history,
worth listening to even if its parts did not hang together
and its narrator was excessively anecdotal for his
scientific side.

When I paused as if approaching the end of the story,
he offered some fresh knowledge to keep me up to date.
"Lately, people have found viruses which may have

something to do with lupus.[66] Just another in a long line of theories," he said. To my questioning look he responded, "Viruses are very tiny and mysterious. They cause some diseases for sure—polio and measles. Other diseases with unknown causes are bound to be linked with viruses sooner or later, since viruses are everywhere." He suddenly stopped as if he had to turn a fresh page in a textbook, then he took some matches from his trouser pocket and lit his pipe. Only after he inhaled deeply several times did he get up from his chair. On his way out he paused by the door and said, "The nicotinic-acid magic—I will try that on some patients, I promise."

On my last day in the hospital, Dr. Alper summed up my status. All my tests were back and were remarkably normal. The LE cells had disappeared. The kidneys were perfect.

"If I had not known the history and seen you in your sicker days, I would not have suspected, much less made the diagnosis of lupus. You must lead a pretty normal life now."

"I am a living example of one of Osler's aphorisms: if you want to live a long life, get a chronic disease and take care of it."

"What are you doing now to take care of it? Whatever it is, it is working and I would not stop it."

"I don't really do very much about lupus anymore. I take my so-called placebo, the nicotinic acid. You have a skeptical smile. But I feel sure that the nicotinic acid has helped me more than anything else. Maybe you will find out someday why it works. Meanwhile, I am not neglecting myself. I eat a good diet, take my vitamins, and sleep eight to ten hours each night. Trying not to get overtired seems to be the main problem now. I want to do so many things. . . . In the past few years I have rediscovered the pleasure of walking and I start the mornings by exercising. I do a few pushups to keep in shape—I call them pushups, but everyone else in the family calls them 'half-pushups.' My days are full of activities, but working with boys and girls like Mildred— that's right, you didn't know Mildred. She helped to nurse me back to health after my gallbladder operation. My experience with her awakened me to the problems that youngsters face with rehabilitation. And . . . I do lots of gardening. I still tend to the flowers in my bare feet. It must be something I have carried over from my ancestors in Europe. Smelling and touching the damp soil has always been a weakness of mine."

"I hope you are careful of the sun."

"Don't worry, I am."

"And drugs, too," he was quick to remind me.

"I know. Even the newest 'miracle drugs' would not tempt me."

NOTES

1. "First do no harm"
2. In 1948 M. Hargraves and his associates reported the presence of an abnormal leucocyte in the bone marrow aspirate from patients with SLE, and its apparent specificity. The cell and its inclusion body were named the "LE cell."
The LE cell is of great diagnostic value in systemic lupus erythematosus. The factor responsible for LE cell formation, in the opinion of some researchers, may play a role in the clinical course of the disease.
M. M. Hargraves, H. Richmond, and R. Morton, *Proc. Staff Meet. Mayo Clin.* 23:25-28, 1948.
3. Newsletter from Manhattan Chapter, Lupus Erythematosus Foundation, Inc. (80 East End Avenue, Apt. 9D, New York, New York 10028), p. 1.
Lupus erythematosus, commonly called "LE" or "lupus," is a widespread, chronic inflammatory disease that involves the connective tissue of the body. Collagen, as this binding substance is called, cements the body cells together and as all organs are composed of cells bound together any breakdown in the cement substance may cause damage to organs such as kidneys, liver, brain, lungs, heart, and also the joints.
4. R. Dubos, *Man Adapting.* (New Haven, Conn.: Yale University Press, 1965), p. 62.
5. B. J. Hoffman, *Arch. Dermat. Syph.* 51:190-192, 1945.
6. P. Cohen and F. H. Gardner, *J. Amer. Med. Assoc.* 197:817-819, 1966.
7. *Ibid.*
8. E. L. Dubois, The clinical picture of systemic lupus erythematosus. In *Lupus Erythematosus,* ed. by E. L. Dubois. New York, McGraw-Hill, 1966, p. 146.
9. Fictitious name.
10. M. Crichton, *Five Patients: The Hospital Explained.* New York, Alfred Knopf, 1970, p. 162.
11. Huang Ti nei ching su won, *The Yellow Emperor's Classic of Internal Medicine.* Chapters 1-34 translated from the Chinese with an introductory study by Ilza Veith. New ed. Berkeley, University of California Press, 1966, p. 184.

12. Cohen and Gardner, *op. cit.*
    S. L. Lee and M. Siegal. Drug-induced lupus erythematosus.
    In *Drug-Induced Diseases*, v. 3, ed. by L. Meyler and H. M.
    Peck. Amsterdam, Excerpta Medica Foundation, 1968, pp.
    239-248.
13. Rachel Carson, *Silent Spring*. Greenwich, Conn., Fawcett,
    1962, p. 170.
14. Dr. Diamond is now Professor of Pediatrics, Emeritus from
    Harvard Medical School and presently Professor of Pediatrics
    at the University of California in San Francisco. He is noted
    for having trained more pediatric hematologists than any-
    one before or since.
    Dr. Diamond discovered new blood groups, new protein
    types, and perfected methods for detecting Rh immuniza-
    tion. He developed the albumin-slide test for detecting Rh
    immunization. He described with Blackfan the syndrome of
    aregenerative anemia of childhood.
15. Since I saw Dr. Diamond, my father has died at the age of
    seventy of arteriosclerosis, and my mother has passed away
    at the age of seventy-four of diabetes.
16. E. L. Dubois and J. D. Arterberry, *J. Amer. Med. Assoc.*,
    181:366-374, 1962.
    D. Alarcon-Segovia and P. J. Osmundson, *Ann. Intern. Med.*
    62:907-919, 1965.
17. Fictitious name.
18. George W. Thorn, M.D., Physician-in-Chief (1942-1972),
    Peter Bent Brigham Hospital, Boston, Massachusetts. Hersey
    Professor of the Theory and Practice of Physic, Emeritus,
    Harvard Medical School.
19. Sack: a popular drink in Holland in the seventeenth century.
20. David McCord, *The Fabrick of Man, Fifty Years of the
    Peter Bent Brigham*. Boston, Pub. for the hospital by the
    Fiftieth Anniversary Celebration Committee, 1963, p. 3.
21. M. Kaposi, *Arch. Dermat. Syph.* 4:36-78, 1872. Kaposi
    reported two patients with discoid (platelike) patches on the
    skin who later became fatally ill, presumably with systemic
    (skin plus internal organs) lupus erythematosus. Throughout
    the literature one reads of many similar accounts. S. C. Gold,
    Lancet 1:268-272, 1951. R. H. More, *Amer. J. Path.* 26:702,
    1950.
22. A low white-cell count is an important feature of LE being
    present in over 60 percent of the cases.
23. S. C. Gold and N. F. C. Gowing, *Quart. J. Med.* 22:457-481,
    1953.
24. Professor Frank H. Gardner, Director of Hematology
    Research, Peter Bent Brigham Hospital (1949-1966), and

Physician-in-Chief, Presbyterian Hospital, Philadelphia, Pennsylvania.

25. Sir William Osler, Canadian-born physician, 1849-1919.

26. D. A. Turner, *Treatise of Diseases Incident to the Skin*, 5th ed., London, 1736, p. 113-14, as quoted by Ole Horwitz. In *Lupus Vulgaris Cutis in Denmark, 1895-1954*. Copenhagen, 1960, p. 3.

27. Certain substances: Creatinine, urea, and other waste products of metabolism which the kidneys must dispose of. The author's creatinine clearance was 10 percent of normal at the time of Dr. Gardner's statement regarding kidney damage.

28. Dubois, *op. cit.*

29. R. H. Moser, Renal Diseases. In *Diseases of Medical Progress: A Study of Iatrogenic Disease*, ed. by R. H. Moser. 3rd ed. Springfield, Illinois, Charles C. Thomas, 1969, p. 569.

30. R. Dubos, *Mirage of Health*. New York, Harper and Row (Perennial Library Edition), 1971, p. 167.

31. N. B. Kurnick, *Arch. Intern. Med.* 97:562-575, 1956.

32. An Associated Press release entitled, "U.S. Curbs Drug Use in Animal Feed," appeared in the *Boston Herald Traveler*, February 1, 1972, p. 2.

33. Cohen and Gardner, *op. cit.*

34. P. S. Hench, E. C. Kendall, C. H. Slocumb, and H. F. Polley, *Arch. Intern. Med.* 85:545-666, 1950.

35. *Ibid.*

36. Nicotinamide is the amide of pyridine 3-carboxylic acid (niacin) $C_6H_6ON_2$. Nicotinamide will produce results comparable in every way to those obtained by use of the free acid. (Eli Lilly and Co., Indianapolis, Indiana.)

37. A. Leslie, *Amer. J. Med.* 16:854-862, 1954.

    S. Wolf, *Res. Pub. Ass. Res. Nerv. Ment. Dis.* 37:147-158, 1959.

    J. B. Knowles and C. J. Lucas, *J. Ment. Sci.* 106:231-240, 1960.

    L. D. Hankoff, *Dis. Nerv. Syst.* 23:39-40, 1962.

38. L. A. Lloyd and J. W. Hiltz, *Canad. Med. Ass. J.* 92:508-513, 1965.

    E. H. Mandel, *New York State J. Med.* 63:3111-3113, 1963.

39. O. Gilje, *Acta Derm.-Venereol* 32:51-55, 1952. (Lupus developed at the site of BCG in a girl of thirteen, who was revaccinated one year after her first vaccination.)

    L. F. Ayvazian and T. L. Badger, *N.E.J.M.* 239:565-570, 1948.

    J. M. Neff, *et al. N.E.J.M.* 276:125-132, 1967.

40. G. A. G. Peterkin, *British Med. J.* 2:1-6, 1945.

41. L. Eiseley, *Amer. Scholar* 35:292, 1966.

42. H. H. Sawicky, N. B. Kanof, M. G. Silverberg, and M. Braitman, *J. Invest. Dermat.* 19:397-404, 1952.

43. F. O'Connor, *Everything That Rises Must Converge*, Introduction by Robert Fitzgerald. New York, Farrar, Straus and Giroux. 1967.

44. H. L. Holley, *Arth. Rheum.* 7:684-686, 1964.
H. Holman, *J. Ped.* 56:109-119, 1960.
H. Holman and H. R. Deicher, *Arth. Rheum.* 3:244, 1960.

45. *Nicobion: Literature über die Therapeutische Anwendung des Nikotinsäureamids.* Darmstadt, Germany: The Merck Company, pp. 14-19.

46. W. H. Auden, "The Art of Healing. (In memoriam Davis Protetch, M.D., 1923-1969)" *New Yorker* magazine, vol. 45, September 27, 1969, p. 38.

47. L. Popoff, M. Popchristoff, and B. Batchvaroff, *Bull. Soc. Franc. Dermat. Syph.* 46:1038-1041, 1939.
L. Popoff, *Bull. Soc. Franc. Dermat. Syph.* 46:1076-1081, 1939.
L. Popoff, *Dermat. Wchnschr.* 113:785-791, 1941.

48. L. Popoff and M. Kutinscheff, *Dermat. Wchnschr.* 116:186, 1943.
L. Popoff, In *Symposium Dermatologorum* (Prague, 1960) v. 1-3. Prague, Universita Karlova, 1962, v. 1, pp. 28-31; v. 3, pp. 27-30.

49. Richard Bright, one of the great clinicians of the nineteenth century, connected the shrunken kidneys at postmortem with the clinical picture of uremia, a deadly kidney disease.

50. E. W. McChesney, F. C. Nachod, and M. L. Tainter, *J. Invest. Dermat.* 29:97-104, 1957.

51. Precipitation of the attacks by cold is common, as in one of Osler's original cases (Osler, 1897).

52. Most doctors' explanations of lupus are characteristically vague; some state the meager facts, giving the impression they know something more concrete.

53. S. E. Ritzmann, and W. C. Levin, *Arch. Intern. Med.* 107:754-772, 1961. A cold sensitivity is called cryopathy in medical language. The term was suggested as an all-inclusive term for clinical conditions associated with cold sensitivity.

54. Kurnick, *op. cit.*

55. E. L. Dubois, *J. Amer. Med. Assoc.* 173:1633-1640, 1960.
E. L. Dubois, *Ann. Intern. Med.* 45:163-184, 1956.

56. Compazine (prochlorperaquin). E. Beutler, R. J. Deren, C. L. Flanagan, and A. S. Alving, *J. Lab. Clin. Med.* 45:286-295, 1955.

57. Demerol (meperidine). P. Nordquist, G. Cramer, and P. Bjorntorp, *Lancet* 1:271-272, 1959.

58. Seconal, (secobarbital). S. Moeschlin and B. Demiral *Acta Haemat.* 8:29-41, 1952.
59. Meprospan (meprobamate). B. C. Brown, E. V. Price, and M. B. Moore, *J. Amer. Med. Assoc.* 189:599-604, 1964.
60. Quote taken from letter from Susan Rosenblum written to author on March 10, 1972.
61. L. Meyler, ed. *Side Effects of Drugs.* v. 5. Amsterdam, Excerpta Medica Foundation, 1966, pp. 269-275.
62. W. Withering, *An Account of the Foxglove and Its Medical Uses, with Practical Remarks on Dropsy and Other Diseases.* London, 1785.
63. Bulgarian remedy-nicotinic acid.
64. A. White, P. Handler, and E. L. Smith, *Principles of Biochemistry.* New York, McGraw-Hill, 1968, pp. 580-581.
65. F. W. Peabody, *Doctor and Patient.* New York, Macmillan, 1930.
66. "Presence of Virus-like Structures Confirmed in Collagen Disease." *J. Amer. Med. Assoc.* 211:761, 764, 1970.

GLOSSARY

ACETAZOLAMIDE:

A sulfonamide diuretic (causes increased urine formation or excretion). Trade name Diamox.

ACROCYANOSIS:

Mottled blue discoloration of the skin of the extremities.

ALBUMIN:

"White protein"; an important protein of human blood serum which may be found in the urine in diseases of the kidney.

ANTIBODIES:

Proteins in the blood and secretions which combine with either native or foreign molecules. They may have a protective or harmful action.

ANTICONVULSANTS:

Drugs used to reduce frequency of convulsions.

ASPIRIN:

In 1763, it was discovered that an extract of the willow bark was effective in relieving the pains of rheumatism. Willow extract owes its therapeutic efficacy to a substance that is called salicylic acid— from the Latin name for willow, *salix*. A chemically modified form, acetylsalicylic

156

acid, is marketed under the name of aspirin. For reasons still unknown, aspirin proves helpful for relieving pain.

AUTOGENOUS VACCINES:

Vaccines which are made from the patient's own bacteria as opposed to vaccines which are made from standard bacterial cultures.

BASAL METABOLISM:

Radioactive iodine uptake. The rate is tested to determine whether the thyroid gland is over- or underactive.

BIOPSY:

A sample of tissue for microscopic study.

BUN:

Blood urea nitrogen. When the kidneys fail, the BUN rises, as does the uric acid.

BUTTERFLY RASH:

A form of double-wing-shaped skin rash around the nose and cheeks indicative of lupus.

CORTISONE:

A potent hormone of the adrenal glands; the pure compound was first discovered in adrenal secretion by Dr. Edward C. Kendall of the Mayo Clinic and by Dr. Reichstein of Basel, Switzerland, simultaneously in 1936. It is now synthesized as a pure chemical.

D AND C:

Abbreviation for "dilation of the cervix and curettement of the uterus."

DIURETIC: A drug that helps to make
                           more urine.

DNA: Deoxyribonucleic acid, a large
                           complex molecule composed
                           of chemicals called sugars and
                           nucleic acids.

DROPSY: The swelling of the legs and
                           abdomen which most often is
                           caused by heart failure, but
                           can be due to kidney or liver
                           disease.

EKG: Electrocardiogram. This is a
                           recording of electrical forces
                           from the heart.

ENDOCRINOLOGY: The study of the glands of
                           internal secretion.

ENZYME: A protein substance that
                           catalyzes a biological or
                           chemical reaction

ERYSIPELAS: A contagious, infectious
                           disease of skin and subcu-
                           taneous tissue, marked by
                           redness and swelling of
                           affected areas and with con-
                           stitutional symptoms.

ERYTHEMA NODOSUM: Painful red bumps on the
                           skin. A skin manifestation of
                           several diseases, including
                           lupus.

FOXGLOVE: A plant whose leaves
                           resemble fingers (digits)

GALACTOSE: One of the sugars in milk, a
                           part of the lactose molecule.

GENETIC:

Pertaining to the genes; the word "genetic" refers to the property of transmission of parental characteristics to offspring.

GI SERIES:

Gastrointestinal series; an X-ray examination of the esophagus, stomach, and small intestine.

HEMATOLOGIST:

A specialist in the study of blood.

HEMATOLOGY ROUTINE:

Tests to count the cells of the blood. The LE cell is a white cell that has eaten the nucleus of another white cell; the latter appears as a blue-staining spot inside the first cell.

HEPATITIS:

Inflammation of the liver.

HISTOPATHOLOGY:

Change in tissues and cells.

HORMONE:

From the Greek "to excite"; hormones are chemical messengers which excite a response in other tissue.

HYDROXYCHLOROQUINE:

Antimalarial drug that has also been used as a suppressant for lupus erythematosus.

HYPERSENSITIVITY:

A form of allergy generally mediated by antibodies, a special group of blood proteins.

IMMUNITY:

The power to resist infection or invasion of bacteria.

INFECTIOUS MONONUCLEOSIS:	A self-limited, probably infectious disease that presents, with fever, upper respiratory symptoms, and swelling of the lymph nodes.
IVP:	Intravenous pyelogram, an X-ray examination of the kidneys.
LEUKOPENIA:	Low white-cell count.
LYMPHS (lymphocytes):	White blood cells.
MEPACRINE:	Quinacrine, Atabrine, the antimalarial drug which was taken by United States Armed Forces personnel during World War II.
MYASTHENIA GRAVIS:	A disease in which nerve impulses are not properly transmitted to the muscle cells. As a result, muscles all over the body become weak.
NICONACID:	Swiss-French trademark for a preparation of nicotinic acid.
PELLAGRA:	A deficiency of niacin, one of the B vitamins, which causes diarrhea, dermatitis, and dementia.
PENICILLIN:	Antibiotic.
PEPSENCIA:	Trade name for a medicine containing stomach digestive enzymes.
PHLEBITIS:	Inflammation of a vein

PLACEBO:

An inactive substance given to a patient either for its pleasing effect or as a control in experiments with an active drug.

PLASMA:

The fluid portion of the blood in which the blood cells are floating.

POLYARTERITIS NODOSA:

Inflammation of the large arteries.

POLYS
(polymorphonuclear
leukocytes):

White blood cells.

PREDNISONE:

The chemical name for a steroid hormone.

PUPILLARY REACTION:

Constriction of the pupil in response to light which may be painful in inflammatory disorders of the eye.

PURPURA:

A disease that is characterized by the rupture of blood vessels with leakage of blood into the tissues.

RHEUMATOID ARTHRITIS:

A chronic disease of the joints.

SEDIMENTATION:

The settling of red blood cells to the lower portion of a volume of blood which has been treated to prevent clotting.

SIDE EFFECT:

An adverse effect produced by a drug. One disorder is being replaced by another.

SPONTANEOUS REMISSION: A change in the course and severity of a disease which occurs without medical intervention.

STREPTOCOCCUS: The round organism (coccus); a very dangerous bacterium that may cause sore throats and skin infections such as nephritis, inflammation of the kidneys, rheumatic fever, inflammation of the heart and joints.

SULFADIAZINE: An anti-infective drug, one of the sulfonamides.

TETRACYCLINE: An antibiotic effective against many of the bacteria which are not affected by penicillin.

THYROID TESTS: Basal metabolism, radioactive iodine intake—tests to determine whether the thyroid gland is over- or underactive.

ULTRAVIOLET: That portion of the spectrum of sunlight which tans the skin.

VASOMOTOR: Pertaining to control of the tone of the blood vessels. Contraction of blood vessels causes blanching, whereas relaxation causes blushing.